Diary of a NICU MOM

A Mother's Story and a Guide to Thriving in the NICU

Nakia Henry

Diary of a NICU Mom: A Mother's Story and a Guide to Thriving in the NICU
Copyright © 2025 by Nakia Henson

This book is a work of nonfiction based on personal experiences. Some names and identifying
details have been changed to protect the privacy of individuals. The author is not a medical
professional; the content provided is for informational and inspirational purposes only and
should not replace medical advice.

ISBN: 979-8-218-79522-1

eBook ISBN:979-8-218-79523-8

Editor: Jenny M.

Cover design by: Kristen Andrews

For Bailey, my miracle. You are my why.

ACKNOWLEDGEMENTS

First and always, I thank God for carrying me through one of the hardest seasons of my life.

To my husband, thank you for being my partner in every sense of the word. You held my hand through uncertainty, reminded me to breathe when fear took over, and stood firm for our family when I felt weak.

To my mom and dad, thank you for being my foundation. Your strength, love, and prayers gave me courage when I didn't have it on my own. Knowing you were there for me and for Bailey brought me comfort I'll cherish forever.

To my family and friends, your prayers, love, and encouragement sustained me more than you'll ever know. Every message, visit, and thoughtful gesture gave me the strength to keep going.

And to Bailey, my miracle, my light, my reason for writing these pages. You are the bravest soul I know, and you have changed me forever. This book is for you and because of you.

Introduction

No one can truly prepare you for the journey of having a premature baby, especially when that journey begins in the Neonatal Intensive Care Unit (NICU). After I delivered Bailey, she was whisked away to the NICU in a flurry of doctors and nurses. I could only steal a few precious seconds with her before she was taken away. The sight of her tiny body, hooked up to myriad machines and monitors, was both reassuring and terrifying. It was a stark reminder of how fragile and precarious her situation was.

As a new mother, I had spent months dreaming of holding my baby close, feeling her warmth against my skin, and bonding with her right after birth. But instead, I could only touch the top of her head before she was taken away. That fleeting moment with my daughter made me realize that this journey would be an emotional rollercoaster unlike anything I had ever experienced or imagined.

Bailey was born at University of Maryland Capital Region Medical Center, which has a level-3 NICU. At the time, I had no idea what that meant or how it would impact our or our baby's care. I felt completely overwhelmed, lost in a sea of medical terminology and unfamiliar procedures. This sense of helplessness led me to do extensive research, not just on NICUs but on every aspect of premature birth and infant care. It was this research, combined with my personal experience, that ultimately inspired me to write this book.

As a NICU mom, I quickly learned that it is crucial to ensure your baby is receiving the best level of care possible. The first question every parent should ask is, "Is this NICU the best fit for my baby's needs?" This question became even more important when we later transferred to a level-4 NICU at Children's Hospital.

In Part 2 of this book, I include a comprehensive NICU Parents' Guide. It was created to help other NICU parents navigate this overwhelming and often confusing journey. While I am by no means an expert, I wanted to share my personal experience, the lessons I learned, and the resources I found helpful. My hope is that it will serve as a beacon of light for others during one of the most difficult times in their lives.

Coping with being a NICU mom was not easy for me. There were days when the weight of uncertainty and fear felt crushing. But I found that writing provided some solace. It became my outlet, allowing me to process my emotions, document our journey, and find meaning in our struggles. This book is the result of countless late-night writing sessions, often penned while sitting beside Bailey's incubator or during the rare moments of quiet at home.

Throughout this book, I will share my personal journey in its entirety—the good, the bad, and the ugly. I won't sugarcoat the challenges we faced or the moments of despair. But I'll also highlight the moments of joy, the small victories that kept us going, and the incredible strength we discovered within ourselves.

My goal is for anyone who reads this book to feel empowered and never give up hope. If you are a NICU parent, I hope this book brings you comfort and reassurance. I want you to know that you're not alone in your fears, your doubts, or your hopes.

Just remember, this journey will not be easy. There will be days when you cry, scream, and feel angry at the unfairness of it all. Some days you will make progress, celebrating milestones you never knew existed before the NICU. Other days might feel like a step back, even up until the day of discharge. The NICU experience is rarely linear, and that's okay.

But know this: You will smile again. You will find strength you never knew you had. You will become an advocate, a medical expert, and a pillar of support for your child. And one day, whether it's weeks or months from now, you will walk out of those NICU doors with your baby in your arms.

So, let's begin with the day that changed everything: March 8th, 2024. The day our NICU story began, the day our lives were forever altered, and the day we learned the true meaning of love and hope in the face of unimaginable challenges.

PART 1: LIFE IN THE NICU

CHAPTER ONE

MORNING OF MARCH 8TH, 2024

I t was a crisp March morning when the pains in my lower back started. I brushed them off, thinking they were nothing more than growing pains. However, these back pains were intense. This was my first pregnancy, so I was unsure of what the pain could possibly be. It originated in my lower back and varied between a dull throb, a constant ache, and sharp jolts. The pain began at around 10:00 a.m., but I pushed through and continued working throughout the day. I even went out with my husband, Bobby, to run errands and grab lunch. In the evening, I went to a "Tea"-making class with my sisters and mom as planned.

Despite the pain I was feeling, I didn't want to cancel our plans. Looking back now, that was the last night when everything felt normal. I was pregnant and looking forward to going on our "babymoon" in a week with my husband. But in just one night, everything changed.

As the evening approached, the pain became unbearable, and I knew something was wrong. We rushed to the hospital, where I was admitted at only 22 weeks and 6 days pregnant. The doctors told me I was already 6 cm dilated, and my heart dropped. This wasn't supposed to happen so soon. Despite my fears and doubts, I put all my trust in God and followed my instincts throughout the entire ordeal.

Over the next few days, I was put on bed rest and constantly monitored by the medical team. Every day felt like a roller coaster of emotions, from hope to fear and back again. But through it all, I held on to my faith and the love of my family and friends. They were my pillars of strength during the toughest moments. As days turned into weeks, I found myself adjusting to my new routine in the hospital. I was getting used to being hooked up to monitors 24/7.

The doctor suggested surgery to close my cervix, so I had cerclage placement surgery on March 11th. I was discharged from the hospital on March 17th and put on strict bedrest. But just three days later, the contractions returned, and I was readmitted to the hospital.

As I lay in the hospital bed, still reeling from the sudden realization that I might give birth prematurely, I was visited by two medical professionals who couldn't have been more different. First, a nurse practitioner entered my room. Her warmth and empathy washed over me while she spoke softly, taking her time to explain the situation and what I could expect from our NICU stay. Her gentle approach provided much-needed comfort in this overwhelming moment.

Then, the attending doctor arrived. Her clinical, matter-of-fact demeanor was a stark contrast to the nurse's warmth. Her rapid-fire explanations were filled with medical jargon, leaving my head spinning. I struggled to keep up with her words, feeling a mix of gratitude for her expertise and frustration at her impersonal approach.

"Would you like a tour of the NICU?" the nurse practitioner asked me gently. I shook my head, unable to find my voice. The thought of seeing those tiny babies fighting for their lives was too much for me to bear at that moment. I needed time to process, to prepare myself for what was ahead.

It's no surprise that, with all this information, I was on an emotional rollercoaster. The nurse's compassion soothed me, while the doctor's blunt delivery served to heighten my anxiety. Yet, at the same time, I felt a growing determination rising within me. I realized that I would need to draw strength from different kinds of support during this NICU ordeal

They quietly exited, leaving me alone with my thoughts and fears. Despite the fear and uncertainty, I steeled myself for what was to come. The contrasting approaches of these two professionals prepared me for the complex journey ahead, each in her own way. As I placed a protective hand over my belly, I whispered a promise to my unborn child: *We're in this together, little one. No matter what comes our way, we'll face it with strength and love.*

Just as I was getting used to my new routine back in the hospital, I started having contractions again. And at this point, on March 22, doctors were unable to give me any more medicine to stop the contractions. So they scheduled me to get my epidural, and because Bailey was head down, I was blessed enough to have a vaginal delivery. My delivery was so peaceful; everyone was quiet and calm. Bailey was born at 24 weeks and 6 days. When she came out, she didn't cry. I was able to touch her head, but she was taken to the NICU quickly. Even though everyone was nervous about the possible outcome of the birth, I was not. I knew she was going be okay. It was just her time to enter this world.

And that was the start of our NICU journey.

As I reflect on that fateful night of March 8th, my mind often wanders to the "what ifs." What if I had chosen to tough it out and not go to the hospital? What if we had gone to a different hospital?

These thoughts bring tears to my eyes because every decision we made that night seemed to be divinely guided. My intuition led me down a path that ultimately saved both my and my baby's lives.

The First 24 Hours

After enduring the intense pain of childbirth, my body finally felt some relief. The lingering effects of the epidural still coursed through me, dulling any discomfort. Bailey was born three-and-a-half months too soon, at twenty-four weeks and six days. The doctors had warned us about the statistics, numbers that haunted my dreams: 60–70 percent survival rate; significant risk of lifelong complications; and weeks or months in the NICU, if she made it at all. But statistics don't account for the fierce determination my family and I had.

I can vaguely recall the doctor coming into my room and delivering the good news: Bailey was doing wonderfully and wouldn't need to be intubated. This brought a wave of immediate relief over me, as all I wanted was to see my baby girl.

I mourned the loss of the birth experience I had dreamed of—the excitement of going into labor and the anticipation of holding my newborn immediately after birth. Instead, I was faced with the prospect of a clinical, emergency delivery and a prolonged NICU stay. Despite my fear, I felt a steely determination growing within me. I may not have chosen this path, but I was ready to walk it with all the strength and courage I could muster. I made a silent promise to my baby and to myself: *I will do whatever it takes to bring you home. We will face this journey together, my little fighter.*

As dawn broke, casting a soft light through the hospital window, I took a deep breath. This was the beginning of our NICU journey—unexpected and challenging, but also filled with hope. I couldn't possibly know what the coming days and weeks would bring, but I knew one thing for certain: My love for my baby would guide me through every step of this unfamiliar path.

Unfortunately, the doctors informed me that it would be a few hours before I could visit Bailey in the NICU. They needed to make sure she was stable and settled in her room. So, while waiting anxiously for my first visit with her, I rested and spent time with family.

Finally, after what seemed like an eternity, I was able to go see my daughter. Still unable to walk on my own, I had to be wheeled down to the NICU unit. As we left the maternity unit and approached the doors of the NICU, a sudden rush of emotions overwhelmed me. I was nervous and unsure of what to expect. Upon arrival at the unit's entrance, we were stopped by security who required our names and ID before allowing us entry. Knowing that there was tight security in place gave me some peace of mind. We then had to be personally buzzed in by the NICU staff by camera before being welcomed into the NICU itself. Immediately upon entering, I was ushered to a hand-washing and sanitizing station and instructed that I must thoroughly wash my hands every time I enter the NICU, a necessary precaution in such a delicate environment.

As I was wheeled closer to Bailey's room, my heart raced with anticipation. I finally opened the door, my eyes immediately filling with tears, and a mixture of joy and sadness washed over me. Joy at seeing my precious daughter for the first time and sadness at knowing that this would be her new home for quite some time. The sight before me was overwhelming—the numerous machines and beeping sounds in Bailey's room and the realization that her tiny body was inside a clear box illuminated by a blue light. I would later learn that this box was called an "incubator"—or, as I lovingly referred to it, Bailey's "spaceship." Designed to simulate a mother's womb, it provided the necessary warmth and sterility for her fragile state.

With the help of the NICU staff, I was brought close to the incubator. Peering through the small doors on the side, I gently placed my finger inside and felt Bailey's tiny hand wrap around it. At only 1 lb. 9 oz., she was incredibly small and delicate yet filled with so much life and fight. Her head was full of soft hair, and she had bushy eyebrows and a cute button nose. She truly was a miracle baby.

However, we were already facing our first setback, within hours of her birth. Bailey needed to be intubated, which I knew was a possibility but had hoped wouldn't be necessary. My heart ached, hoping that her premature lungs would be strong enough to thrive without any assistance from machines.

As I gazed at my newborn daughter lying in the NICU incubator, a wave of reality hit me like a ton of bricks. I couldn't believe that this was happening to us, that our baby had arrived so unexpectedly and was now fighting for her life.

I stared at her delicate face, attached to tubes and wires, and tried to remember whether there had been any signs that this would happen. Any indications that my body wasn't strong enough to carry her to full term. My mind raced with memories of my pregnancy.

I remember the day and time I found out I was pregnant: October 27th, 2024, at 11:39 a.m. I checked early that morning, and the test said I wasn't pregnant. I went to an event with my sister that morning. I was extremely tired and didn't want to stay at the event for long, so we left around 10 a.m. to head home. I told myself I wouldn't keep checking to see if I was pregnant, but I went to the bathroom and decided, okay, let's check again. *I peed on the stick and waited a few minutes to check. And the digital test came back and said "Pregnant." I told myself not to get too excited; maybe it was just a false reading. But I took two more tests after that, and they all said the same thing. I was thrilled but also still in shock; I had convinced myself that I couldn't get pregnant, so this was a dream come true.*

Telling your spouse that you are pregnant is such an overwhelming experience. I wanted to make sure I told Bobby at the perfect time. I came up with so many ways I wanted to tell him I was pregnant. Since I found out about a week before our wedding anniversary, I wanted to wait until then to talk to him, but holding this kind of secret was too much for me. However, I could at least wait until I ordered gifts for him, telling him he would be a dad. So about two days later, I left a box for him on the kitchen table, waiting to surprise him when he walked in. Inside the box were about four positive pregnancy tests, a onesie that read "Hello Daddy," and a few other gifts. He was in shock but so happy. It is a day I will never forget.

I was so excited about the pregnancy that I couldn't wait for my first doctor's appointment. I wanted to see my baby and make sure everything was okay. My first appointment was scheduled for November 17th. When the day finally came, I was bursting with excitement. I wasn't experiencing any weird symptoms or complications, so I assumed everything was fine. My husband and I walked into the office and were greeted by a friendly nurse who took my vitals and asked me a few questions. Then came the moment I had been waiting for: the ultrasound. Seeing my baby's tiny form on the screen, his or her little heart beating, was a feeling I can't describe. I was in awe of this little life growing inside of me. The doctor came in and confirmed that everything looked good, that I was six weeks pregnant and the expected due date was July 6th, 2024.

From the moment I found out I was pregnant, I had envisioned a smooth and uneventful pregnancy, just like in the movies, where laughter and glowing skin were the norms. But reality hit me hard, crashing like thunder, and I was forced to face the relentless storms of a high-risk pregnancy. Each day felt like a battle; I was overwhelmed with nausea that swirled in my stomach like a tempest, followed by waves of vomiting that left a metallic taste in my mouth. Gestational diabetes wrapped around me like a heavy fog, while exhaustion made sleep feel perpetually out of reach. The only sanctuary I found was in the warm embrace of the shower, where the steaming water cascaded over my skin, washing away the aches and bringing a fleeting sense of relief that enveloped me like a gentle hug. Yet, little did I know, the sickness and tormented nights were merely a prelude to even greater trials that awaited me in the months to come.

CHAPTER TWO

MEETING MAY AND AMANDA

I sat in the dimly lit NICU, the beeping of monitors my constant companion. I was struck by the profound loneliness of
this experience. Despite the flood of text messages and phone calls
from well-meaning friends and family, I felt isolated in a way I had
never imagined possible. Their words of support, while appreciated,
couldn't bridge the gap between their world and mine.

It felt like time stopped for me while the rest of the world moved
on. Days blended into nights, and I found myself losing track of hours,
sometimes even forgetting to eat. Other days, I couldn't stop eating,
as if filling my stomach might somehow have filled the emptiness I felt
inside.

Sleep became a luxury I couldn't really afford. When I did close my
eyes, my dreams were filled with the sounds of alarms and the sight of
my tiny baby, so fragile in her isolette. I would awaken in a cold sweat,
reaching for my phone to check if there were any updates from the
night nurse.

In this sterile, medical environment, I yearned for a connection that went beyond the surface-level understanding of my situation. I needed someone who truly got it, someone who had walked in these same hospital-issued slippers and felt the weight of uncertainty pressing down on their chest.

That's when I realized the importance of finding a "person." Not my husband, not my mom, but another NICU mom. Someone who understood the conflicting emotions of hope and fear that waged war in my heart every day. Someone who knew what it was like to celebrate the tiniest of victories, like a few grams of weight gain or a slight decrease in oxygen support.

As I looked around the NICU, I could see other mothers, their eyes carrying the same mix of exhaustion and determination that I felt. I made a mental note to reach out, to perhaps form a bond over our shared experience. Because having someone who truly understands, someone who's fighting the same battle, can make all the difference.

This NICU experience taught me about a different kind of strength, a resilience I never knew I had. It also showed me the power of connection, even in the most isolating of circumstances. As I turned back to watch my daughter's tiny chest rise and fall, I made a promise to myself: I would find my "person," and together, we would navigate this challenging, beautiful, heartbreaking journey of NICU motherhood.

As I look back on my NICU journey, I'm struck by how pivotal finding my people was to my survival and sanity during those long, challenging months. The NICU can be an isolating place, a world apart from the normal flow of life, but that is where I forged some of the strongest connections I've ever known.

May

I remember the day I met May as if it were yesterday. It was just another day of entering the NICU, a routine that had become as familiar as breathing. I was waiting in line at the front desk, my mind preoccupied with thoughts of Bailey's progress and the day ahead, when I turned to the woman next to me and asked, almost on autopilot, if she also had a baby in the NICU. Her affirmative answer was the beginning of a friendship that would become my lifeline.

May and I clicked instantly. We shared not just a last name, but a depth of experience that only fellow NICU parents can truly understand. She had given birth at 28 week and, like me, had endured a long and traumatic hospital stay. As we began to share our stories, I felt a weight lifting off my shoulders. Here was someone who understood the rollercoaster of emotions, the technical medical jargon, and the unique challenges of NICU life.

Our friendship blossomed quickly. We exchanged numbers and soon were in almost daily contact. I found myself looking forward to our coffee dates, our conversations a mix of sharing advice, venting frustrations, and celebrating small victories. We even found humor in comparing notes about the different nurses and doctors, finding comfort in our shared observations and experiences.

Amanda

But the universe wasn't done gifting me with support. Just a week after meeting May, I encountered Amanda in the NICU lounge area. Her story left me in awe—she had gone into premature labor while visiting her son's father's family in Maryland, far from her home in

New Jersey. The strength it must have taken to navigate the NICU experience alone, in an unfamiliar city, was staggering to me.

Amanda's situation made me acutely aware of my blessings. While I struggled with the daily commute to and from the hospital, at least I had the comfort of my own bed each night. Amanda was living in the hospital, making do with the recliners in the NICU room. Her partner could only visit every other weekend due to work commitments, leaving her to face the bulk of this ordeal alone.

As I reflect on these friendships, I'm filled with gratitude for the way they transformed my NICU experience. May and Amanda became my tribe, my support system in a world that often felt incomprehensible to those on the outside. We shared tears and laughter, fears and hopes. We celebrated each gram of weight gain, each reduction in oxygen support, as if they were Olympic victories.

These women taught me the true meaning of resilience. May's determination during her long NICU stay inspired me to keep pushing forward on my toughest days. Amanda's courage in navigating this challenging time so far from home reminded me of the incredible strength we can find within ourselves when we have no other choice.

Our bond went beyond just sharing similar experiences. We became each other's confidantes, therapists, and cheerleaders. When the weight of worry threatened to overwhelm me, a text or call from one of them could lift my spirits. When I doubted my ability to handle another day of uncertainty, their support and belief in me restored my confidence.

Looking back, I realize that finding "my people" in the NICU was not just about having someone to talk to. I was able to find a community that understood this unique experience, a support system that could empathize with the specific challenges we faced. May and

Amanda weren't just friends; they were fellow warriors in the trenches of the NICU battle.

Our friendships deepened as our NICU stays progressed. We celebrated milestones together, comforted each other during setbacks, and shared the bittersweet emotions of eventually leaving the NICU. Even after our discharge dates, our bond remained strong. We had been through an experience that changed us profoundly, and our connection reflected that transformation.

Now, as I look at Bailey thriving at home, I often think of May and Amanda. Our shared NICU experience created a sisterhood that transcends time and distance. We keep in touch, sharing updates on our children's progress and reminiscing about our time in the NICU.

Finding my people in the NICU was a silver lining in a difficult situation, and it was a crucial part of my journey. May and Amanda helped me find strength I didn't know I had, offered perspectives I hadn't considered, and provided comfort that no one else could. They were, and continue to be, an integral part of my story as a NICU mom.

I'm filled with immense gratitude for these unexpected friendships. They remind me that, even in our darkest moments, connections can be forged that light our way forward. May, Amanda, and I are more than friends. We're NICU sisters, bonded by an experience that shaped us all, supporting each other long after we left those hospital walls behind.

New Routine

The first 30 days in the NICU were an emotional rollercoaster, but we gradually settled into a new normal day by day. Every morning, I awoke at 6:36 a.m., the exact time Bailey was born. This ritual became sacred to me, a moment to center myself before facing another day in the NICU.

I'd begin each day with a heartfelt prayer:

Dear God, I thank you for the life of my newborn baby. Thank you for bringing her into this world and for giving me a chance at motherhood. Father, I dedicate my baby to you. She came too soon, and I can't take her home yet. I pray that just as you took care of her when she was inside me, You continue to protect her in the incubator. Please give her everything she needs to survive. Guide and protect her from any sickness or infections. Fill her with strength and help her grow healthy in Jesus' mighty name. Amen.

After my prayer, I'd call the night nurse for an update on Bailey's progress. These calls were comforting; I dreaded potential bad news but was always eager to hear about any improvements, no matter how small. Once I got my report, I'd shower, dress, and head to the hospital, my mind already racing with thoughts of Bailey and the day ahead.

The NICU's strict visiting policy was challenging. Only my husband and I were allowed regular visits, with two additional visitors permitted for the entire NICU stay. This restriction saddened me deeply, as it meant our extended family wouldn't meet Bailey until she came home. Choosing which two family members would be allowed to visit was an agonizing decision. We ultimately decided on both our mothers, but made sure our fathers and siblings could FaceTime with Bailey daily, sometimes multiple times a day.

What truly helped us through this difficult time were the relationships we formed with the nurses. We quickly identified our favorite nurses, those who went above and beyond in their care for Bailey and support for us. Conversely, there were nurses we weren't as fond of, those who seemed detached or robotic in their approach. While no one ever mistreated Bailey, the difference between a nurse who was passionate about their job and one who was just going through the motions was stark.

One nurse in particular, Angela, was like an angel sent to us. She was Bailey's nurse during our first week in the NICU, and was the one who made me comfortable touching Bailey for the first time, ensuring I was involved in her care from the start. She educated me about my rights as a NICU parent, emphasizing that my voice was not only mine but Bailey's, too. Angela encouraged me to speak up if something didn't feel right and assured me there were no stupid questions in the NICU.

Our daily routine became a well-choreographed dance. I'd arrive at the NICU and go straight to Bailey's room, greeting the morning nurse. Then I'd wait for morning rounds, when the medical team would discuss Bailey's progress and plan for the day. After rounds, I'd grab a quick coffee before returning to Bailey's room to sit with her for hours. I loved being with her, reading her stories, or just watching her tiny chest rise and fall with each breath.

Lunchtime would come and go, which I rarely would notice as I remained fixated on Bailey. I'd typically stay until the night nurse started their shift, making sure to greet them and discuss the plan for the evening before reluctantly heading home.

This routine became our new normal, but it wasn't without its challenges. The constant beeping of monitors, the clinical smell of the NICU, and the emotional toll of seeing our tiny daughter fighting for her life all weighed heavily on us. Yet, we found strength in the small victories: a gram of weight gained, a slight reduction in oxygen support, or a moment of eye contact with our precious girl.

We also found unexpected moments of joy and connection. The camaraderie among NICU parents was a source of comfort. We'd share stories in the family room, exchange knowing glances in the hallway, and offer words of encouragement to those having particularly tough days. These connections reminded us that we weren't alone.

As the days turned into weeks, we became more confident in our roles as NICU parents. We learned to read Bailey's monitors, understand medical terminology, and advocate for her needs. We decorated her space with photos, small toys, and inspirational quotes, transforming the sterile hospital environment into a more personal, loving space for the routine we'd established. Each day brought new challenges and triumphs. We celebrated milestones like Bailey's first full feed, her first time breathing without assistance for a few minutes, and the first time we were able to hold her without a tangle of wires and tubes.

Through it all, our love for Bailey grew exponentially. The NICU experience, while incredibly difficult, also gave us a unique opportunity to bond with our daughter in ways we never anticipated. Every diaper change, every temperature check, every gentle touch became an act of love and devotion.

As we approached the one-month mark in the NICU, we reflected on how far we'd come. The fear and uncertainty of those first days had given way to a cautious optimism. We knew the road ahead would still be long and challenging, but we felt more prepared to face it. Our tiny warrior had already shown us her incredible strength and resilience, and we were committed to matching it with our constant love and support.

Little did we know, our NICU journey was about to take an unexpected turn, testing our newfound strength in ways we couldn't have imagined...

CHAPTER THREE

THE NIGHT OF THE TRANSFER

May 2nd, 2024, began like any other day in the NICU. I awoke at 6:30 a.m., said my morning prayers, and called the hospital for my daily update on Bailey. After receiving the report, I went through my usual routine of showering, dressing, and making the short drive to the hospital.

During morning rounds with the doctors, we discussed the day's plans as usual. However, I couldn't shake a nagging feeling of unease. Bailey's stats were dropping more frequently than normal. While this wasn't entirely uncommon—we often had to adjust her CPAP machine settings—something felt different today.

When Bobby arrived at the hospital at the end of the day, he spent some time with Bailey before suggesting we grab dinner and head home. I was reluctant at first; leaving Bailey's side always filled me with anxiety. But seeing her having an "okay" day, I agreed, planning to call and check on her before deciding whether to go straight home.

As we pulled up to the restaurant, exhaustion hit us both. We decided to get our food to go instead. Just a few minutes down the road, my phone rang. It was the hospital's number, and my heart plummeted. In the NICU world, "no news is good news" was our motto. A call, especially in the evening, could only mean something was wrong.

With trembling hands, I answered. The nurse's voice was calm but serious: "Hello. Bailey is okay, but I think it's time for her to be transferred to another hospital." She explained that Bailey's oxygen levels were consistently staying in the 80 range. While this could be okay under normal circumstances, Bailey was on maximum CPAP settings. At full support, she should have been at 100%, so this deviation from her norm was concerning.

The medical team had run a battery of tests and taken X-rays. The results showed Bailey's lungs looked cloudy, indicating she needed to start steroid treatment and use a machine for inhaled nitric oxide, a treatment for babies experiencing hypoxic respiratory failure, particularly those with pulmonary hypertension. This treatment helps relax and expand blood vessels in the lungs, improving oxygen flow to the brain and other vital organs.

Our current hospital didn't have the necessary equipment for this treatment. We were given two options for transfer, both to level-four NICUs. After careful consideration, we chose Children's Hospital in Washington, DC. Although it meant increasing our commute from 7 minutes to 30, I had confidence in this hospital. As a former employee, I knew of their excellent reputation—they were ranked in the top- five NICUs nationwide. I felt a hospital dedicated solely to children, with top specialists, was the best option for Bailey.

The next few hours were a whirlwind of activity and emotion. We rushed back to the hospital, our dinner forgotten. The sight of Bailey, small and vulnerable amidst a tangle of tubes and wires, brought tears to my eyes. The gravity of the situation hit me anew. Our little fighter was facing yet another challenge.

When the transfer team arrived, I felt a mix of fear and hope. Fear of the unknown, of the risks involved in moving our fragile daughter. But also hope that this move would provide Bailey with the advanced care she needed. I watched, my heart in my throat, as they carefully disconnected her from the familiar machines and prepared her for transport.

Bobby and I followed the ambulance to Children's Hospital, the 30-minute drive feeling like an eternity. We held hands in silence, each lost in our own thoughts and prayers. Arriving at the new NICU was overwhelming—new faces, new machines, new protocols to learn. But as we watched the team efficiently settle Bailey into her new space, we felt a glimmer of relief. This was where she needed to be.

That night, we reluctantly left Bailey in her new surroundings. While we were leaving, we reflected on how quickly things can change in the NICU. Just that morning, we thought we were on a steady path. Now, we were facing a new chapter in our journey, one filled with new challenges but also new hope.

As we drove home, exhausted but determined, I silently renewed my promise to Bailey. *No matter what comes our way, we'll face it together.* This unexpected turn was just another part of our story, another hurdle we'd overcome. With the support of this new medical team and our love, I knew Bailey would continue to fight and thrive.

Little did we know, this transfer was just the beginning of a new phase in our NICU journey, one that would test our resilience in ways we never imagined, but also bring unexpected blessings and growth.

The first day in the new NICU at Children's Hospital was a whirl-wind of emotions and experiences. We didn't leave until 2:30 a.m., finally arriving home at 3:00 a.m., exhausted but determined.

Additionally, today marked the end of my short-term FMLA leave. The transfer couldn't have happened at a worse time. I had been on leave since I first went into the hospital in March. I didn't want to use my actual Maternity leave yet, until Bailey was home, so I had to return to work. Luckily, my job as an IT Project Manager is 100% remote, so I could work while at the hospital. My job can be intense at times, especially when projects are close to deadline, so working and watching over Bailey at the hospital was going to be challenging.

The 30-minute drive each way was already proving strenuous, and we quickly added finding temporary accommodation in the city to our growing to-do list.

The differences between our old NICU and this new one were immediately apparent and somewhat overwhelming. Gone was our private room; we now shared a space with three other families. This new arrangement was a double-edged sword: On the one hand, it meant constant activity and noise, but on the other, it provided a sense of community and shared experience that was oddly comforting.

The sheer size of the new NICU was staggering. We had gone from a cozy 15-room unit to a sprawling 70-room level-4 NICU. The increased capacity meant more resources and specialized care, but it also felt more impersonal at first. We had to navigate new corridors, learn new protocols, and familiarize ourselves with a much larger medical team.

One feature that stood out was the video surveillance in Bailey's room. This 24/7 access was both a blessing and a curse. While it provided immense relief, especially during those late nights at home, it also tugged at my heartstrings to see Bailey alone in her crib. I used it sparingly to maintain my emotional balance.

Adjusting to the new medical team presented its own set of challenges. Bailey was now assigned to the Nurse Practitioner team, which meant a whole new approach to her care. During rounds, we'd be surrounded by an NP, an attending physician, a social worker, a nutritionist, a respiratory therapist, and Bailey's assigned nurse for the day. The wealth of expertise was reassuring, but the sheer number of people involved in her care was initially overwhelming.

Despite the challenges, there were unexpected bright spots. On our second day, the hospital hosted an event for families on the rooftop. Bobby and I reluctantly attended for a few minutes, taking pictures with an oversized photo frame and props. Those brief moments of fresh air and normalcy were a welcome respite from the intensity of the NICU.

As the days passed, we began to appreciate the support Children's Hospital could offer. They had resources and programs for families that our previous NICU hadn't provided. Support groups, counseling services, and even small events like the rooftop gathering all contributed to a more holistic approach to NICU care.

We also started to form connections with the other families in our shared room. There was an unspoken understanding between us, a bond forged through shared experiences of fear and hope. Late-night conversations while tending to our babies became a source of comfort and strength.

The medical care at Children's was truly top-notch. Bailey's new treatment plan, including the nitric oxide therapy, was closely monitored and adjusted. We watched in awe as the team worked tirelessly to stabilize her condition. Their expertise and dedication were evident in every interaction, every adjustment to her care plan.

As we settled into our new routine, we found ourselves constantly balancing hope and anxiety. Each small improvement in Bailey's condition was cause for celebration, while every setback tested our resolve.

The emotional rollercoaster of NICU life continued, but now with new twists and turns.

One particularly challenging aspect was maintaining our connection with family and friends back home. The increased distance and our exhausting schedule made it difficult to keep everyone updated. We started sending group texts and occasional video updates to bridge the gap, but it was hard not to feel isolated at times.

By the end of our first week at Children's, we had begun to find our footing. We were learning the rhythms of this new NICU, forming relationships with the staff, and most importantly, seeing small but steady improvements in Bailey's condition. The road ahead was still long and uncertain, but we felt more equipped to handle whatever challenges came our way.

As we looked back on that first chaotic day of transfer, we realized how far we'd come in such a short time. Our little warrior continued to amaze and inspire us with her strength and fortitude. This new chapter in our story was teaching us valuable lessons about adaptability, perseverance, and the importance of community support.

With each passing day, we grew more confident in our ability to familiarize ourselves with this new environment. We were no longer just parents in crisis mode; we were becoming advocates, partners in Bailey's care, and sources of support for other NICU families. Our story had taken an unexpected turn, but we were rising to meet the challenge, buoyed by hope and love for our tiny fighter.

As we entered our first week at Children's Hospital's expansive 70-room NICU, I felt both overwhelmed and hopeful. The sheer size of the facility was daunting, but I knew we were in one of the best places for Bailey's care. During our second week at Children's, our luck turned when Jen, one of our first nurses, recognized our dedication to spending time with Bailey, and put in a request on our behalf to the charge nurse to be moved to a private room. The new room was considered "prime real estate" due to its large window, rarity in such a large facility.

I'll never forget the moment we stepped into that room. The stunning view of the city from the 6th floor took my breath away. As I stood by the window, cradling Bailey in my arms, I felt a mix of emotions. The solitude was comforting and a welcome change, but I couldn't help but miss the sense of community we'd experienced in the shared room. It was a bittersweet realization; the isolation allowed us to focus entirely on Bailey, but it also emphasized the gravity of our situation.

During those first few days in our private room, I became acutely aware of the diverse circumstances other NICU families faced. It was a shock to learn that not all parents could visit daily, with some managing only weekend visits or evening check-ins. This realization brought a renewed sense of gratitude for our ability to be present consistently for Bailey. I cherished every moment by her side, knowing how precious this time was.

CHAPTER FOUR

ADJUSTING TO THE NEW NORMAL

A djusting to the new NICU was a process. Each day brought new challenges as we familiarized ourselves with the larger facility and worked to build relationships with the expanded medical team. I spent hours poring over information about the advanced equipment and protocols at Children's Hospital, determined to understand every aspect of Bailey's care. It was overwhelming at times, but I drew strength from the knowledge that we were giving Bailey the best possible chance.

Just as we were settling into a routine, a close friend offered us accommodation a few minutes from the hospital. I can't describe how relieved I felt. The daily commute had been taking its toll, and the thought of being so close to Bailey lifted a weight off my shoulders. Packing up our lives into a few suitcases was surreal. We were about to make DC our home for the next five months, all for the love of our tiny fighter.

The temporary relocation brought a whirlwind of emotions. There was a sense of displacement as we left our home and support system behind, but also a feeling of purpose in being closer to Bailey. I found myself constantly balancing gratitude for our new situation with homesickness for the familiar. To cope, we developed strategies to maintain connections with family and friends from afar. Weekly video calls, daily update texts, and sharing photos became our lifeline to home.

However, our world expanded further when we learned we could add two more people to our visitor list, bringing the total to four. The day both grandfathers finally met Bailey in person was incredibly emotional. Watching them interact with her face-to-face, rather than through a screen, was a moment I'll treasure forever. The depth of connection in those interactions was profoundly different from our previous FaceTime calls. I saw the love and wonder in their eyes as they gazed at their tiny granddaughter, and it filled my heart with joy.

As the days passed, I noticed our confidence as NICU parents growing. We became more assertive in asking questions, more involved in decision-making, and more adept at reading Bailey's cues. The nurses often commented on our dedication, and I felt a sense of pride in our ability to advocate for our daughter.

Bailey's progress was slow but steady. Each small milestone—a gram of weight gained, a slight reduction in oxygen support, a moment of eye contact—felt like a victory. I meticulously documented every change and every achievement in a journal. It became my way of processing our experience and holding onto hope during the challenging days.

One particularly memorable moment came when Bailey was strong enough for her first kangaroo care session. While I held her against my chest, skin-to-skin, I felt an overwhelming surge of love and connection. In that moment, all the machines, alarms, and medical jargon faded away. It was just me and my daughter, bonding in the most primal way.

As we approached the end of our first month at Children's Hospital, I reflected on how far we'd come. We had adapted to a new environment, formed relationships with an incredible medical team, and most importantly, watched our daughter grow stronger each day. The road ahead was still long and uncertain, but I felt more prepared to face whatever challenges came our way.

The NICU had become our new normal, a place where hours blended into days, and days into weeks. It was a place of fear and hope, of heartache and joy. But above all, it was the place where our daughter was fighting her hardest battle, and we were determined to be there every step of the way.

As I tucked Bailey in for the night, whispering words of love and encouragement, I realized that this experience had changed us immeasurably. We were no longer just parents; we were warriors, advocates, and partners in Bailey's care. And though the future remained uncertain, one thing was clear: Our love for our tiny fighter would guide us through whatever lay ahead.

CHAPTER FIVE

PRIMARY NURSES

A few weeks after our transfer to Children's Hospital, our NICU experience took a significant turn for the better. It was an ordinary day when a young nurse entered Bailey's room, introducing herself as our daughter's caregiver for the shift. But what she said next filled us with unexpected joy—she had signed up to be Bailey's primary nurse. Her name was MG, and little did we know how much of a blessing she would become.

The concept of a primary nurse was something we had longed for at our previous NICU, where the policy of rotating nurses left us feeling anxious and disconnected. We had our favorite nurses there, of course, but the constant change in caregivers was a source of stress. Each new nurse meant a learning curve—understanding Bailey's unique needs, her feeding schedule, medication regimen, and the little quirks that made her comfortable.

MG's decision to become Bailey's primary nurse was a game-changer. It meant consistency in care, a familiar face who would truly get to know our daughter, and a reliable point of contact for us.

The relief we felt was immense, knowing that even when we couldn't be at the hospital, there would be someone who cared deeply for Bailey watching over her.

But the blessings didn't stop there. Just a few days later, we were introduced to Deysi, who also expressed her desire to be Bailey's primary nurse. Both MG and Deysi expressed that they had fallen in love with our little fighter and wanted to be part of her care team for the duration of her stay. Their commitment touched us deeply, and we felt our daughter's support system growing stronger by the day.

Bailey was such a playful baby; she always smiled brightly, especially whenever someone looked into her incubator. Her tiny lips would curve into a smile that lit up her entire face, despite all the tubes and tape covering it. When my dad would visit, he would whisper to me, while leaning over her incubator, his hands pressed against the clear plastic, "I know this may sound crazy, but I swear this little girl understands every word we say."

I understood why he felt that way. Sometimes during rounds, the attending physician, while reviewing her chart, said things like, "Most premature infants won't overcome respiratory distress without long-term complications," or "It's doubtful she'll be weaned off oxygen this quickly." But the very next day, Bailey would be breathing more steadily, her oxygen saturation numbers climbing on the monitor like a quiet rebellion.

Toward the end of our NICU stay, one of the biggest challenges we had with Bailey was feeding; she couldn't finish a whole bottle. She would get so tired midfeed, and for her to be discharged from the NICU, she had to finish close to 80% of each bottle. It seemed like it was not going to happen for her because she was only averaging 30–40% of each bottle. After a few weeks of working on her bottle feeding, the doctors wanted us to consider giving Bailey a G-tube, which is a feeding tube that would require Bailey to have surgery. We were told that we had to make this decision soon because it was the only thing keeping Bailey in the NICU, and there was nothing else medically holding her back. The other option was to put her in a rehabilitation center to continue working on feeding. However, two days later, Bailey started taking 100% of her bottle. It was as if she heard us and said, "Okay, got it. Watch me work."

She was nothing but a ball of pure determination wrapped in a hospital-issue blanket. That's why I treasured MG and Deysi so much. They recognized that fierce spirit in her. While other nurses saw charts and protocols, they saw Bailey, really saw her, and that recognition meant everything to Bobby and me during those endless NICU days.

Having primary nurses brought a new level of comfort and stability to our NICU experience. We noticed how MG and Daisey quickly picked up on Bailey's subtle cues—the way she preferred to be positioned, the times of day she was most alert, and the techniques that soothed her during procedures. This intimate knowledge of our daughter's needs and preferences meant more consistent, personalized care.

The benefits extended beyond just Bailey's immediate care. MG and Daisey became our partners, offering insights into Bailey's progress that went beyond mere medical data. They celebrated her milestones with genuine excitement, comforted us during setbacks, and provided emotional support that only those intimately involved in Bailey's care could offer.

Their presence also allowed us to step away from the NICU with less anxiety. Knowing that Bailey was in the hands of nurses who knew her so well gave us the courage to take much-needed breaks, even if just for a quick meal or a short walk outside. This respite was crucial for our mental health and allowed us to return to Bailey's side refreshed and recharged.

The relationship we developed with MG and Deysi went beyond the typical nurse-patient dynamic. They became confidantes, cheerleaders, and an integral part of Bailey's story. We found ourselves sharing not just medical concerns but also our hopes, fears, and dreams for Bailey's future. Their compassion and dedication made the sterile environment of the NICU feel more like a nurturing space where our daughter could thrive.

As the weeks passed, we witnessed firsthand the impact of having primary nurses. Bailey seemed to respond differently to their care; she was more relaxed and more engaged. We noticed subtle improvements in her condition that we attributed, at least in part, to the consistency and attentiveness of MG and Deysi's care.

Their influence extended to us as parents as well. MG and Daisey took the time to educate us, encouraging us to be more involved in Bailey's care. They taught us how to read her monitors, understand her cues, and perform care tasks with confidence. This knowledge not only helped us feel more in control of the situation but also prepared us for the day we would finally take Bailey home.

The introduction of primary nurses marked a turning point in our NICU journey. It transformed our experience from one of constant uncertainty to one of partnership and shared commitment to Bailey's well-being. MG and Deysi became more than just nurses; they became part of Bailey's extended family, integral characters in the story of her early life.

We felt immense gratitude for this unexpected blessing. The nurses' dedication reinforced our belief that we were in the right place for Bailey's care. Their presence was a constant reminder that even in the most challenging circumstances, there are always people willing to go above and beyond, to love and care for our children as if they were their own.

My Friend Is Back

As I continued to settle into our new routine at Children's Hospital, I couldn't help but reflect on the saying that "everything happens for a reason." It had been heartbreaking to leave behind the support system I'd built at our first NICU, especially my friendship with Amanda. We had connected instantly, bonding over our shared NICU experiences, and her absence left a void in my emotional support network.

But, just a week after our transfer, I received surprising news: Amanda's son was also being transferred to Children's Hospital. My emotions were conflicted; I was thrilled to have my friend and support system back, but deeply concerned for Amanda and her son. I knew all too well that a transfer often meant a worsening condition requiring more specialized care.

Amanda's arrival at Children's was bittersweet. Her familiar face eased my transition to this new, overwhelming environment. We quickly fell back into our supportive friendship, now navigating the challenges of a larger, more advanced NICU together. Amanda's presence helped me feel less isolated, and I found comfort in our shared understanding of this unique experience.

We resumed our routine of sharing information about NICU procedures, comparing notes on our babies' progress, and offering each other emotional support during tough moments. Our late-night conversations in the family lounge, shared meals in the hospital cafeteria, and the comfort of having someone who truly understood the NICU rollercoaster became my lifeline.

As we faced the ups and downs of our babies' medical ordeals together, our friendship deepened. Despite the challenging circumstances, I found a silver lining in our reunion. Amanda's support and understanding helped me adjust to our new environment with greater optimism and hope.

Looking back, I realized that while this time was incredibly challenging, unexpected blessings could emerge. My rekindled friendship with Amanda was proof of that. Her presence reminded me that even in the darkest times, there was light to be found, sometimes in the form of a friend who understands what you're going through like no one else can.

Chapter Six

Journal Entries

On Day 68, I made a decision that would greatly impact my experience and ultimately shape this book: I began keeping a daily journal. The NICU can be an overwhelming whirlwind of medical jargon, emotional highs and lows, and critical decisions. I often struggled to keep track of Bailey's progress, the myriad information thrown at us daily, and my tumultuous emotions. That's when I turned to writing.

My journal became more than just a record of events; it evolved into a helpful tool that served various purposes throughout our NICU stay. First and foremost, it became my memory keeper. In the sleep-deprived, stress-filled days of the NICU, important details often slipped through the cracks. By meticulously documenting every aspect of Bailey's care—from medication changes to feeding schedules, from doctors' rounds to nurse observations—I created a comprehensive record of her journey. This not only helped me stay informed but also taught me how to ask more pertinent questions and actively participate in her care decisions.

The journal also became my emotional outlet. Some days, the pages were tear-stained as I poured out my fears and frustrations. Other days, they were filled with joy and hope as I celebrated small victories—a gram of weight gained, a reduction in oxygen support, or a moment of eye contact with Bailey. Writing allowed me to process these intense emotions in a healthy way, preventing them from overwhelming me during critical moments of Bailey's care.

Unexpectedly, my journal also became a source of strength and perspective. On particularly challenging days, when progress seemed slow or setbacks occurred, I found solace in flipping back through earlier entries. Seeing how far Bailey had come and remembering obstacles we had already overcome provided much-needed encouragement and renewed my hope. It was a tangible reminder of our strength and Bailey's fighting spirit.

As time went on, I began to include more than just medical updates and emotional reflections. I started documenting the small, precious moments that made our story unique—the first time I got to change Bailey's diaper, the day Bobby and I sang to her together, the moment she wrapped her tiny hand around my finger. These entries became treasured memories, snapshots of love and connection amidst the clinical environment of a hospital room.

I also used the journal to keep track of questions for our medical team, ideas for making Bailey's space more personal, and plans for her eventual homecoming. It became a central hub for all things related to our NICU experience, helping me stay organized and focused during a time when it was easy to feel scattered and overwhelmed.

Looking back, I realize that this daily practice of journaling did more than just help me make sense our NICU stay. It laid the foundation for this book. The detailed accounts, raw emotions, and personal reflections captured in those pages have allowed me to share our story with authenticity and depth. It's my hope that by sharing these journal entries, other NICU parents will feel less alone in their journey and perhaps be inspired to start their own NICU journals.

To all NICU parents reading this, I cannot stress enough the value of keeping a journal during your NICU stay. It doesn't have to be elaborate or time-consuming. Even a few lines each day can make a significant difference. Your journal can be whatever you need it to be—a record keeper, an emotional outlet, a source of strength, or all the above. In the challenging and often unpredictable world of the NICU, your journal can be a constant companion, a silent witness to your journey, and a record of your strength and love for your child.

As we jump into the next section of this book, which contains my personal journal entries starting from Day 68, and ending on Day 192, when Bailey finally came home, you'll see firsthand how this practice evolved and the impact it had on our NICU experience. These entries are raw, unfiltered, and deeply personal. They capture not just Bailey's medical journey, but our emotional journey as parents during such a unique and life-changing experience. Through these pages, I invite you to walk alongside us, to share in our challenges and triumphs, and to find hope in our story.

CHAPTER SEVEN

Day 68: May 29

Morning: I woke up at 6:30 a.m. and resolved to make changes today. My first task was to wash Bailey's old and new crib sheets, along with her beloved stuffed octopus and blanket. I also tossed out the wilted flowers from the baby shower we had thrown and washed the vases they were in. I hailed a Lyft to get to the hospital, since my car had been parked there overnight.

Afternoon: May came to visit today. She had an appointment for her daughter at Children's Hospital. Bailey has been desatting more than usual today. I'm not sure why, but it's concerning. The doctors adjusted her settings, and I can only pray that is the cause of her increased desatting.

On the drive home, I found myself praying fervently. "Dear God," I whispered, "please watch over Bailey tonight. Give her strength, stabilize her breathing, and let her know how deeply she is loved. Guide the hands and minds of her caregivers, and grant us all a peaceful night."

Day 69: May 30

I woke up feeling frustrated and overwhelmed. Bailey had caught a virus exactly a week ago, and it seemed like she was getting better—her oxygen requirements were decreasing. But then suddenly, in one day, her oxygen needs doubled. It felt like all the progress we had made since transferring to Children's Hospital was reset.

It was too much for me to handle in one day, so I took a break. I went home, turned on the TV, started a new series, ordered Mexican food, and did some coloring. I needed some time for myself, away from the constant beeping of machines. It helped ease my mind a bit.

Day 70: May 31

I woke up in a good mood today. But as I was on my way to the hospital, my husband called me with news that Bailey had to be put back on the nitro oxygen machine and was requiring 100% oxygen support. It felt like my happiness was taken away in an instant. I went from dancing in the car to crying.

After listening to rounds, the doctors reassured me that Bailey would get back on track soon, but it would take time. This virus had triggered underlying issues for Bailey, which was why we had come to this hospital in the first place. Tomorrow, Bailey will be 35 weeks old. I couldn't be prouder of her—she is the strongest person I know.

Day 72: June 2

The sun was shining bright, a perfect start to the day. We were filled with excitement as we loaded up into a luxurious van and headed to the winery with our close friends. The first stop was at the same beautiful winery I had visited for Mother's Day. It was such a long ride. At any other time, I would complain about sitting for so long, but I was just happy to be surrounded by friends and to have an adult conversation, taking my mind of the NICU.

After some time at the first winery, we hopped back on the sprinter van and made our way to a second one. As we sipped on various wines and enjoyed each other's company, I couldn't help but feel grateful for this moment away from the hospital. It had been a while since we had done something fun with a group of friends, ever since Bailey was admitted to the NICU. After leaving the second winery, we went back to our friends' house for pizza. But as much as we tried to enjoy ourselves, there was a lingering sense of worry and guilt.

We left our friends' house and headed to the hospital. When we arrived, the nurse informed us that Bailey had had a good day, but just shortly after we arrived Bailey desatted at least ten times. And I'm not talking about just going down to the 80s and 70s; I'm talking about going down to the 40s and dropping her heart rate. They had to bag her several times, and she was on 100% oxygen requirements.

Watching a bunch of doctors and nurses run into your baby's room to literally save their life is traumatizing. Even after they stabilized Bailey and left the room, I couldn't move. I was in shock. How did was go from such a beautiful day at the winery to such an evening of sadness?

It was a long and tiring night, and when she finally settled down for the night, I could feel my emotions overwhelm me. My heart ached for her, and I would have traded places with her in an instant. As soon as I got into the car, I cried hard, so hard I couldn't stop, making myself physically sick. Bobby was so worried he had to stop the car.

We had been dealing with Bailey's diagnosis of rhinovirus for over a week now, learning that it was a common occurrence in the NICU—like a common cold for babies. We just had to get through this hurdle, which I knew we would, but it was such a scary time. My nerves were on edge.

Day 73: June 3

Despite the events of the previous night, we managed to have a good day today. Bailey seemed to do well during the daytime, giving us hope for her recovery.

Bobby and I spent most of our day at the hospital, from 8:30 a.m. to 9:30 p.m. We found a new spot to sit and enjoy our lunch. trying to find some semblance of normalcy in this chaotic time. We were able to bring her oxygen requirements down to 86%, a small victory. However, at night, she went back up to 100% and received her first dart injection. The ups and downs of her condition were beginning to take its toll on us both emotionally and physically. But we knew we had to stay strong for Bailey's sake.

Day 74: June 4

As I approached the entrance of the NICU, I greeted the front desk staff with a smile and a wave. By now we were familiar with one another. The ladies at the front knew my name: "Good morning, Mrs. Henry," they always said with so much warmth. I know it's their job, but their greeting me by name always made me feel good when I arrived.

Walking down the hall, I nodded to the other parents I'd come to recognize over the weeks. We shared a silent understanding, our eyes conveying both empathy and encouragement. As I turned the corner to Bailey's room, my heart lifted at the sight of a familiar face—MG, Bailey's primary nurse, was back on duty.

When I arrived at room, I paused at the sink, methodically washing my hands, the routine now second nature after countless visits.

MG's presence brought an immediate sense of relief. Her gentle smile and confident demeanor had been a constant source of comfort during our NICU journey. As I approached Bailey's incubator, MG was already there, her experienced hands carefully adjusting Bailey's position.

"Good morning," MG greeted warmly. "Someone's been waiting for her mama."

I leaned in, taking in the sight of my tiny fighter. Bailey's chest rose and fell with each breath, the soft beep of monitors keeping time with her heartbeat. Despite the tubes and wires, she looked peaceful, her tiny fingers curled into fists, something she did a lot.

MG began updating me on Bailey's night—her oxygen levels, feeding schedule, and how she responded to her last diaper change. As she spoke, I marveled at how much medical jargon I now understood, a testament to how much we'd learned in our time here.

"Would you like to hold her?" MG asked, already knowing my answer.

With practiced ease, we worked together to transfer Bailey from the incubator to my arms. This was not an easy task—we had to make sure the chair was close enough to the incubator so the cords were not pulling or easy for anyone to trip over. Then we had to make sure we had enough pillows and blankets and put everything I needed within arm's reach. It was always recommended to do skin-to-skin contact for at least an hour at a time. Bailey did not react well to quick holds. As I settled into the rocking chair, Bailey's warmth against my chest, I felt a wave of emotions wash over me. The fear and uncertainty that had been my constant companions seemed to recede, if only for a moment.

MG busied herself around us, checking monitors and making notes, but her presence was comforting rather than intrusive. She had a way of anticipating our needs, whether it was adjusting a pillow or offering a word of encouragement.

As the day progressed, I started to open up to MG about my fears and hopes. She listened attentively, offering both practical advice and emotional support. Her years of experience in the NICU had given her not just medical expertise, but a deep understanding of the emotional journey parents like us were on.

When it was time for Bailey's feeding, MG guided me through the process with patience and encouragement. Every small task I could do for Bailey felt like a victory, a step closer to the day we could take her home.

As the day was coming to an end, I found myself reluctant to leave. MG sensed my hesitation and offered a reassuring smile. "She's in good hands," she said, gently squeezing my shoulder. "You've done a great job today. Get some rest, and we'll see you tomorrow."

Leaving the NICU that evening, I felt a renewed sense of hope. The presence of Bailey's primary nurse had not only ensured the best care for my daughter but had also provided me with much-needed emotional support. The past few days had been rough. It was a powerful reminder of the importance of consistency and familiarity in the often-unpredictable world of the NICU.

As I drove home, I reflected on how much the NICU staff, especially nurses like MG, had become an extension of our family.

Day 75: June 5

I allowed myself to sleep in a little longer this morning, knowing that Bailey had a good night, according to MG when I called at 3am. When I finally made my way to her room, I couldn't help but feel a twinge of disappointment when I saw that her nurse today was not MG, her primary nurse. Perhaps she called out sick or got reassigned to another baby. Either way, today Bailey had two nurses who had never cared for her before. I observed them closely, looking for signs of their "vibes" with Bailey. So far, they seem kind and gentle, their smiles warm as they interact with her fragile body. As a mother, that is all I can ask for—someone who will treat my child with calmness, kindness, and a genuine smile on their face.

Day 76: June 6

When I called the hospital this morning to check on Bailey, I felt like I was holding my breath because I was so nervous about what the update was going to be. Deysi answered and gave me an update—Bailey was at 97% on the ventilator, a sign of progress. For the past few days, we had been starting at 100% each day and working our way down, only to end up back at 100% by nightfall. But today was different. She had made incredible strides overnight.

In a moment of inspiration, I made the decision to fast for the next 30 days, ending on Bailey's due date, July 6th, 2024. I would give up two of my favorite pastimes—watching court shows on YouTube and listening to music while driving. The only music I would allow myself to listen to during this time would be gospel music.

Bailey's nurse today grew up in my hometown, and we graduated from the same high school, though she graduated a few years before I did. For some reason, this relaxed me. At first, I didn't know if I was going to like her because she didn't introduce herself or speak right away when she came into Bailey's room before started working on her. I had to ask, "Are you Bailey's nurse?" But she explained to me that she had been at Children's Hospital since she graduated from nursing school, and was very well experienced and knowledgeable nurse.

Tonight, I had plans to meet with my friend Bianca and her friend, whose son was born premature. I was looking forward to the comfort of talking to someone who had gone through a similar experience.

I firmly believe that prayer is the answer to everything, and I will always share with others what God has done and continues to do in my life. Today was a testimony of that—we started at 97% and made our way down to an impressive 74%. Bailey's primary nurse MG was her evening nurse tonight, giving me peace of mind as I went home to get some much-needed sleep. By early morning, when I called, she had made even more progress and was now at 68%.

Day 77: June 7

Kristen was Bailey's daytime nurse, her gentle voice and warm smile adding a sense of comfort to me today. We had another good day, with Bailey's progress hitting 58%. It was also my husband's grandfather's birthday, and with a light heart, I left the hospital around noon, to celebrate his birthday over lunch. I spent rest of the afternoon picking out thoughtful Father's Day gifts for Bobby and our dads.

Day 78: June 8

Bailey's daytime nurse was Mary Jane. Mary Jane had attended to Bailey during her second day at Children's Hospital. I couldn't tell if Bailey remembered her, but the fleeting smiles exchanged between them felt familiar and warm. It was a wonderful day; Mary Jane managed to bring Bailey's FIO2 down to an astonishing 31%! It was my dad's birthday today, and we went to the movies and had lunch with him, along with my mother and sisters, to celebrate. Even though I was having a great day, I enjoyed the film; however, I randomly started crying at the lunch table. That was happening to me often. I cried almost every day. I could be having a great day, then out of nowhere start crying. I don't know if it was postpartum or the weight of the NICU or both.

But amidst it all, I felt happiness knowing my dad enjoyed his birthday gift. As we were leaving out of the restaurant I also stumbled upon a cute little children's clothing boutique. It became a new little tradition for me: Every time I was out, I would look for something to get Bailey. Even though I knew she couldn't use or wear half the stuff I bought, it made me feel like a "normal" mom buying clothes for her baby. I selected two adorable outfits for Bailey.

Day 79: June 9

Thirty-five percent. I walked into Bailey's room, super proud of her. Bailey had finally come off the nitric oxide machines, a major milestone for a premature baby. Now, at 36 weeks, she could officially be diagnosed with bronchopulmonary dysplasia (BPD), which meant she would have a specialized team working on her twice a week.

Bailey also started feeds again today. It had been about two weeks since she her previous feeds, so we started her off slowly, with just 4 ml every four hours, carefully monitoring her progress.

A few hours later, while Bailey was sleeping, I sat and scrolled on social media. I don't know why I did this myself when I had been highly emotional the past few days. Social media can be hard to process and watch, and I was comparing myself to other moms who were still pregnant, when I should have been, or to people outside who were simply enjoying the start of the summer—knowing I would most likely spend the entire summer at the hospital. I had to remind myself that the time would come soon when I would enjoy my time with my daughter.

CHAPTER EIGHT

Day 80: June 10

Tonight, I finally escaped back to our kitchen. Oh, how I had missed this. We had been surviving off fast food, take-out, and hospital cafeteria food since March. It felt good to be back in the kitchen, cooking a home-cooked meal. I love cooking; I've always poured my soul into cooking, and Bobby was definitely starving for an authentic meal. I made lasagna and a garden salad. I also devoured two glasses of red wine, even though I knew I would regret it later and have heartburn the rest of the night.

It's terrifying how fast life can be stolen from you. Before the hospital, I was religious about cooking; I would cook 3–4 times a week without fail. Then suddenly, everything changed, and I just stopped cooking.

Day 81: June 11

Bailey was making great progress. She had been holding steady with the FiO2 at 30%. Today was eye exam day, and there was nothing new to report. She had a stomach ultrasound (they wanted to rule out a possible stomach infection). They saw something on the X-ray that set our hearts racing, uncertain whether it was stool or an infection, but it turned out it was nothing. THANK GOD! Today was also the first day the BPD team came to see her. They checked her settings with experienced eyes and left with encouraging words, not having any concerns now. Bailey was strong. MG, one of Bailey's primary nurses, had a birthday this week, so, after spending a few hours at the hospital, I left to go find her a gift. I had grown to love the Hallmark store; it was my new favorite place to get gifts. I got her a decorative wine glass that said, "Best Nurse Ever" and two cards, one from Bobby and me, and one from Bailey.

Day 82: June 12

As I walked through the hospital doors and into Bailey's room this morning, my heart skipped a beat at the sight before me. Bailey was now on Fi02 21%, a significant decrease from her previous settings. It continues to amaze me every day to see her progress.

The medical team informed us that they were transitioning Bailey out of her isolate and into a crib. This was a big milestone for her journey toward recovery. They also mentioned that they were weaning her off the breathing tube and lowering her settings even more. If she continues at this rate, they hope to remove the tube by Friday.

I couldn't help but feel overwhelmed by everything that still needed to be done to prepare for Bailey's homecoming. The house needed to be made ready for her arrival, and I knew that God would only grant my prayers if I was prepared to receive them.

Day 83: June 13

I stepped into Bailey's room, and I was overwhelmed with joy to see my baby girl still in the reassuring 20% FiO2 range, sitting at 23%. Today marked her first day out of her incubator! They put her into a "transition incubator"; it's not covered, but it is still temperature-controlled. This was a significant achievement for her, a massive accomplishment. She had spent 83 days in that thing! She needed to spend at least one day in the "transition incubator" while maintaining her body temperature. If she passed this test, they could move her into a standard crib.

I plan to go home after rounds so I could wash clothes I'd been avoiding, clean the kitchen (we barely used it), and gather any trash so Bobby could take it out. And I also needed to bring Bailey some fresh blankets and sheets. Yes, the hospital provided them, but I loved the cute decorative sheets I got her with the matching swaddle wrap. Things like this helped me cope with being in the NICU; it gave me a sense of control.

I also needed to put together everyone's Father's Day gift.

Day 84: June 14

Yesterday was not a bad day for Bailey. However, my day didn't start off so great. I guess I was disappointed because I thought they were going to remove the breathing tube yesterday, but based on several tests, they decided to hold off. So my emotions got the best of me. Compared to last Friday, she had made such a huge difference, so I needed to work on continuing to look at the positive things.

After rounds, they decided to remove the breathing tube! My biggest concern wasn't that she needed the breathing tube; I didn't want it to cause any more damage to her lungs. She looked uncomfortable at times, and I wanted her to be as comfortable as she could be. I believe the more relaxed you are, the more you allow your body to heal on its own.

We had dinner with friends, and had such a great time. We went to this speakeasy in DC for drinks then went to a steakhouse for dinner. This was kind of a "pre–Father's Day" celebration for Bobby and his good friend Josh. That night, we asked our dear friends Josh and Kenya to be Bailey's godparents. Bailey's godfather, his heart filled with humor and loyalty, reminded me so much of my dad, while sweet Kenya radiated warmth, already embodying the love I knew she would give Bailey every day. My heart swelled with excitement for the loving family we were creating around our little girl.

Day 85: June 15

The milestone of 37 weeks finally arrived! We were now just three weeks away from reaching full-term, Bailey's original due date of July 6th, 2024. Today, as I walked into the NICU, I was met with a heartwarming sight: Bailey had been extubated, and her Fi02 was down to 21%, while her oxygen saturation remained at a healthy 100%. My heart swelled with joy and gratitude.

In celebration of this momentous day, I decided to go on a picnic with my family. The weather was perfect—not too hot, not too cold. With our picnic baskets filled with delicious sandwiches, snacks, and refreshing drinks, we made our way to my favorite waterfront spot. We spread out our picnic blankets and gazed up at the clear blue sky, watching planes fly by overhead. The gentle breeze and warm sun lulled us into a peaceful nap; we all were sleep for at least an hour. it truly was the ideal day for a picnic.

As we packed up and left for some ice cream afterward, I couldn't help but feel excited for the summer ahead of us. This simple day spent with my loved ones helped me momentarily forget about the challenges of being a NICU mom.

Later that evening, I returned home to prepare for Father's Day, grateful for the happy memories created on this special day.

Day 86: June 16

Father's Day! It was such a beautiful day. Bobby had been incredibly supportive during the past few months, and I had been on an emotional rollercoaster since the beginning of our NICU stay. But Bobby remained strong for me. He would never let me see him cry. That's one of the things I love about him—not the fact he doesn't cry, but the fact he always puts himself before others. He is such a kindhearted person. No one can ever say anything bad about Bobby. Because he had been so supportive toward me, I wanted to make sure his first Father's Day was special. I took the family to Top Golf and a had really nice time. We played games and ordered food. I couldn't help but smile as I watched my loved ones laugh and bond over this unique experience.

Everyone loved their gifts. Giving gifts is my love language. Especially gifts I know people value and cherish. My Favorite gift was a blown-up picture of Bobby holding Bailey for the first time, and the custom air freshers with Bailey's face

After we left minigolf, Bobby and I decided to treat ourselves to some infused ice cream from a local spot called Tipsy. The indulgent flavors melted in our mouths as we walked together, savoring every moment together.

But the happiness of the day was slightly dampened when we learned that Bailey's primary nurse for the next five days would be someone new. At first, I was hopeful for the consistency of having a daytime nurse for Bailey after so long with rotating shifts. However, as soon as she walked into the room, I sensed there might be some issues. She exuded a carefree persona, not rushing to attend to beeps or alarms like our previous nurses did. It was a complete contrast to what we were used to—nurses who sprinted into the room at any sign of trouble.

Despite this, I appreciated how she made me feel comfortable about changing and holding Bailey whenever I wanted. But my unease grew when she brushed off my concerns about the numbers on the screens and disregarded my questions about the medical plan for the day. Her words—"you focus on her, let me worry about the screens"—made me feel uneasy. It was clear that our communication styles were vastly different, and I knew it would be a challenging five days ahead. However, through this experience, I learned to trust in Bailey's resilience and not panic at every little moment. And for that, I was grateful.

Day 87: June 17

As I entered Bailey's room this morning, the soft light illuminated a scene that filled my heart with a mixture of joy and cautious hope. For the first time since her birth, Bailey was no longer confined to the tiny incubator that had been her home for weeks. Instead, she lay peacefully in a "big girl" crib, her small body looking almost lost in the newfound space.

I approached the crib, my eyes drinking in every detail of this new milestone. Bailey's chest rose and fell with each breath, and I marveled at how she seemed to flourish in her new surroundings. It was a tangible sign of progress, a step closer to normalcy in our NICU journey.

As I stood there, watching my daughter, I heard a commotion from the room next door. The family there was preparing to take their baby home. The sounds of their joy and excitement echoed through the quiet hallways, a bittersweet reminder of the goal we all shared in this place. I felt a pang of envy, quickly followed by guilt for feeling that way. Every baby here had their own unique story—some born prematurely like Bailey, others facing different complications. Yet we were all united in our hope for the day we could walk out of these doors with our little ones in our arms.

I turned my attention back to Bailey, gently stroking her tiny hand. Just three days ago, she had been switched from the NIPV machine to CPAP. I remembered the mixture of fear and excitement I felt as the doctors made the change. Now, as I watched her lying peacefully under the gentle flow of air from the CPAP set to 10, I felt a surge of pride. Her Fio2 numbers were stable, another small victory in our ongoing battle.

As the day wore on, I found myself reflecting on our journey so far. Each day brought new challenges, but also new triumphs. Bailey's strength seemed to grow with each passing hour, and I clung tightly to the hope that soon, we too would be making that joyful journey home.

The nurses came and went, checking Bailey's vitals and adjusting her equipment. I watched their skilled hands at work, grateful for their expertise and care. They had become like family over these long weeks, sharing in our worries and celebrating each small step forward.

As evening approached, I reluctantly prepared to leave for the night. Leaving Bailey was always the hardest part of my day, but I took comfort in knowing she was in good hands. I leaned over the crib, whispering words of love and encouragement to my little fighter.

Walking out of the NICU, I paused to look back at the room where Bailey lay. The sight of her in that big-girl crib, no longer confined by the walls of an incubator, filled me with renewed hope. We still had a long way to go, but today had shown me that progress was possible. With each passing day, we were one step closer to bringing our little girl home.

As I drove home, my mind was already on tomorrow, wondering what new developments it might bring. But for now, I allowed myself to bask in the joy of today's milestone. In the world of the NICU, every step forward was worth celebrating, and today, we had taken a big one.

Day 88: June 18

My parents came to visit, bringing with them a burst of excitement and joy that filled the room. They always had a way of making me laugh, and their concern for my well-being was evident.

As usual, Tuesdays were busy in the NICU. Bailey had several scheduled visits from specialists—the optometrist, physical therapist, and the BPD team. One by one, each specialist made their rounds and provided updates on Bailey's progress.

The most anticipated visit was from the optometrist, who would conduct an eye exam. A few weeks ago, Bailey had been diagnosed with Stage 2 Retinopathy of Prematurity (ROP), a potentially serious eye disease that can occur in premature babies or those weighing less than 3 pounds at birth, both of which described Bailey. ROP occurs when abnormal blood vessels grow in the retina.

But today, there was good news. After the exam, the doctor announced that Bailey was now at stage 0—a huge improvement! Her next follow-up would be in two weeks instead of weekly.

In addition to this positive update, Bailey also made progress in her treatment. She had been transitioned down to a CPAP of 9 from her previous CPAP of 11. The goal was to get her down to a CPAP of 5 before moving onto the Vapotherm machine, a gentler alternative to CPAP that operated on a countdown setting starting at 5 and gradually decreasing to 1. And after that, she would finally be breathing room-temperature air, something that seemed so far away but gave us hope that it would arrive sooner than expected.

Day 89: June 19

Bailey's crib and rocking chair were delivered. My dad went to our house to let the delivery guys assemble the chair and crib, and he also helped clean up. He made such a big difference with his small act.

I went home after being at the hospital all day. I needed a break. However, it wasn't the relaxing moment I had thought it would be. Our air conditioner stopped working, and it was 90 degrees outside. I couldn't enjoy my food and catch up on my TV shows as much because I was too hot and sweaty. But did enjoy just sitting at home. Eventually, I caved and bought a fan, which provided some comfort.

In moments like these, I couldn't help but think back to simpler times when I had no worries or responsibilities. My life had changed drastically since Bailey arrived early and was admitted to the NICU. It was hard to imagine my previous carefree life before spending endless days by Bailey's side in the hospital.

CHAPTER NINE

Day 90: June 20

Bailey's progress continued—she was now on CPAP of 8. The morphine had been stopped, and she was now fully relying on formula for her nutrition. It seemed like a lot of changes for her in just one day, but the medical team closely monitored her to see how she responded.

Despite the changes, I managed to capture some beautiful photos of Bailey today. She looked so vibrant and content, and it brought me joy to see her thriving. I decided to spend another night at my own home to take care of some personal tasks and have a bit of time for myself on Friday.

Day 91: June 21

I started my morning with a visit to the nail salon, pampering myself with a manicure and pedicure. Afterward, I stopped by Old Navy and picked out some fresh summer outfits. And then I made a trip to my new favorite gift shop, the Hallmark store, to find a special gift for our kind friend who let us stay at her city house for an easier commute.

I am truly grateful for her generosity in opening her home to us during this challenging time. I found the perfect gift that I knew she would love, and she did.

Later that evening...

As much as we hoped for continued progress, Bailey's body seemed to struggle with all the recent adjustments. It was suggested that we go back up to CPAP of 9 and give her body some time to adjust before attempting further changes. Her oxygen levels were fluctuating, and she needed more support than usual. So we took a step back and will try again in a few days, always keeping a close eye on her well-being.

Day 92: June 22

Bailey reached her three-month milestone today. If she were still baking in my belly, I would have been thirty-eight weeks, getting ready to deliver Bailey in two weeks. I couldn't believe how fast time had flown by. To celebrate, I took some photos of her and shared them online, feeling a sense of joy as the positive comments from friends and family poured in.

Later that day, I spent time with my mom, dad, and sister. It was our second weekend hanging out together and it felt like a much-needed break from the constant hospital visits. We went to the pool, enjoyed a leisurely lunch, and even went bowling.

As evening approached, I made my way back to the hospital to spend time with Bailey. The routine of going back and forth between home and the hospital had become second nature to me.

Day 93: June 23

It was such a beautiful Sunday morning. I went to go pick up Amanda from the hospital. I knew she could use the fresh air as well. Unlike me, she had been confined to the hospital 24/7 and without transportation to leave, even if she wanted to. After picking her up, we went on some errands together. Our first stop was to pick up paint for Bailey's nursery, a project that had been on my mind for weeks.

After successfully completing our task, we decided to treat ourselves to a hearty breakfast before heading back to the hospital. As we ate and talked, I couldn't help but realize how much I was learning about Amanda. Hearing about all the challenges she faced in her life truly made me appreciate all the blessings in mine.

I discovered that both of her parents had passed away from cancer, leaving her with little family support. She struggled financially as well, with no stable income and her son's father worked a lot, so she was dealing with the NICU issues on her own. Despite these obstacles, she showed resilience by downloading apps that allowed her to make extra money at jobs like being a secret shopper. Her determination and strength were admirable and humbling to witness in person.

Day 94: June 24

As Monday dawned, I felt a renewed sense of hope and determination. The NICU experience had taught me to appreciate every small victory, and today brought a significant one. Bailey's gas levels had improved, allowing her to be put back on CPAP at level 8. This transition from more intensive respiratory support to CPAP was a positive step, and I allowed myself to feel cautiously optimistic.

Throughout the morning, I watched Bailey closely, monitoring her response to the CPAP. Her first day back on this support system went remarkably well. Her tiny chest rose and fell with a steadier rhythm, and the numbers on her monitors remained encouragingly stable. Each hour that passed with Bailey tolerating the CPAP felt like a small triumph.

As the day progressed, I reflected on our journey so far. The roller-coaster of emotions, the countless hours spent by Bailey's side, the medical terminology that had become part of my daily vocabulary—all of it had shaped me into a different person than I was before entering the NICU. I realized how much strength I had found within myself, strength I never knew I possessed.

In the afternoon, feeling more confident about Bailey's status, I decided to take a short break. The nurses encouraged me to step out for a while, assuring me they would contact me immediately if anything changed. With some trepidation, I left the hospital to catch a movie: *Inside Out 2*.

As I sat in the dark theater, I became fully engrossed in the story. The film, a heartwarming coming-of-age tale, resonated deeply with me. It explored themes of growth, change, and the complex emotions that come with facing life's challenges. In many ways, it mirrored my own emotional journey in the NICU.

The movie's portrayal of how joy and sadness can coexist, how difficult experiences can lead to personal growth, struck a chord with me. I saw parallels between the protagonist's journey and my own—navigating unfamiliar territories, facing fears, and finding strength in unexpected places.

As the credits rolled, I felt a sense of catharsis. The movie had given me a much-needed emotional release, allowing me to process some of my own complex feelings about our NICU experience. I left the theater feeling uplifted and rejuvenated, with a renewed perspective on our journey.

Returning to the hospital, I felt a mix of anticipation and calm. The break had done me good, allowing me to return to Bailey's side with fresh eyes and renewed energy. To my relief, the nurses reported that Bailey had continued to do well on the CPAP in my absence.

As I settled back into my chair beside Bailey's incubator, I felt a profound sense of gratitude. Gratitude for Bailey's improvement, for the dedicated NICU staff, for the moments of respite that allowed me to recharge, and for the inner strength I was discovering day by day.

I spent the evening talking softly to Bailey, sharing with her my experience of the day and the movie. Though she couldn't respond, I liked to think that she could sense my presence and draw comfort from my voice. While I watched her sleep peacefully, her monitors showing stable readings, I allowed myself to hope—hope for more days like this, hope for Bailey's continued progress, and hope for the day we would finally bring her home.

Day 95: June 25

This morning, I had a heart-warming conversation with Maddison's mother. I used to watch Maddison when she was just a baby, and now she is entering high school. It's hard to believe how fast time flies. Memories of her as an adorable infant flooded my mind, and I felt a sense of closeness to her that never faded over the years.

Maddison's mother reached out to me on social media to share some news: Maddison had also been a premature baby, born at just 22 weeks. My heart swelled with emotions as I learned this information. I had no idea about her early start in life, but it only made me admire her strength even more. She spent over 90 days in the NICU, fighting for every breath and overcoming every obstacle in her path. And here she is today, a beautiful young lady starting high school.

As I reflected on this unexpected connection between us, a thought crossed my mind. Could it be that God brought Maddie into my life all those years ago because He knew that one day I would have a premature baby of my own? Perhaps He wanted to show me that I am fully capable and prepared to care for Bailey because I already took care of Maddie. The realization brought tears to my eyes and filled my heart with gratitude.

Later that night, Bobby and I attended our regular therapy session. We have been going to therapy for a few weeks. Bobby suggested that we should talk to someone to help us through this current phase we were in. Initially, I hesitated and avoided the topic of speaking to a therapist. I wasn't ready to tell my story or discuss how I was feeling. But Bobby asked me to try it at least once, and I'm glad I did. It was very therapeutic.

Our ongoing struggles were tough, but talking to someone helped us work through our issues and strengthen our relationship. Afterward, I went home, determined to tackle some projects around the house. I started with the nursery and our bedroom, because I knew these spaces needed attention before Bailey arrived.

However, my evening was soon met with an emotional twist when I called the hospital to check on Bailey's progress. In the background, I could hear her crying softly. My heart sank with sadness and guilt as I wished I could comfort her in person. But I knew she was in good hands, and that gave me some peace of mind.

Day 96: June 26

I awoke to find myself just as emotionally drained as I was the night before. My body felt heavy, my mind foggy and overwhelmed with anxiety. The constant cycle of hospital routines had worn me down, and all I wanted to do was stay in bed and sleep away the exhaustion. But I forced myself to push through, determined not to let my anxiety take control.

Surprisingly, despite my fatigue, Bobby and I were invited to spend a few days at the beach in Delaware to celebrate a friend's birthday. The thought of spending some time away from the hospital and enjoying the sunshine lifted my spirits. I longed for a break from the daily stress and a chance to laugh until my belly hurt. Luckily, my parents would be here on Friday and Saturday to watch Bailey so we could enjoy ourselves without worry.

Day 97: June 27

Today marked a milestone for us: We were officially going down to a CPAP of 7! This was a big deal as we had never gone below a CPAP of 8 before. Her gas levels were great this morning, giving us the confidence to make the adjustment. Thankfully, MG, her primary nurse, will be back tonight, which brings me a sense of relief knowing my girl will be well taken care of.

But it was also an exciting day because we were headed to the beach! The salty sea air and warm sand under our feet would be a welcome change from the sterile hospital environment. Finally, a chance to relax and breathe in some much-needed fresh air amidst this journey filled with ups and downs.

Day 98: June 28

The warm sun beat down on the beach, welcoming us to our first full day of vacation in a long, long time. I was grateful that we arrived the previous night so we could secure a room for ourselves, a cozy second-floor space with a large bathroom. The women in our group woke up early and took charge of breakfast, preparing a delicious spread for us all to enjoy. After our meal, we lounged on the deck outside, soaking up the sun's rays and indulging in some much-needed relaxation. Some of us read books, others dozed off to the soothing sound of music playing in the background.

I tried not to call the hospital and my parents too much, but I couldn't help it; I called them a bunch of times. Every time I called, they reassured me that Bailey was fine, and I needed to go and enjoy myself. Which I did, but I couldn't stop thinking about her. I guess this is what it's like being a mother. You are always going to worry about your kids, no matter what.

Eventually, it was time for dinner on Rehoboth Beach's famous boardwalk. We chose a seafood restaurant, and I opted for oysters as an appetizer and steak and lobster for my entrée. While the steak left something to be desired, the lobster was quite tasty. Would I return to this place? Probably not.

After dinner, we made our way to a nearby bar where karaoke night was in full swing. I didn't participate, but it was entertaining to listen to those who did bravely take the stage.

As the night ended, we headed back to our beach house. Exhausted from the day's activities, I quickly showered and fell asleep as soon as my head hit the pillow.

Day 99: June 29

The next day was all about relaxation. We had a huge breakfast before heading to the beach, where we lounged for hours, soaking up the peaceful atmosphere. However, even amidst all this tranquility, my mind couldn't help but wander back to my daughter.

Though it brought me peace knowing she was in good hands, it also tugged at my heartstrings to think of someone else holding her besides myself or Bobby. But I knew I had to let go of my overprotective nature and trust that everything would be okay. MG sent me updates throughout the evening, which helped ease my worries.

It was hard to be away from her, but I also knew it was important for my own mental health and marriage to take this time away. So, I pushed those feelings aside and focused on enjoying the peacefulness of the beach with my friends and Bobby.

Day 100: June 30

I got up early, and wanted to hit the road as soon as we were dressed and packed. I wanted to make sure we got to the hospital early because today was a significant day: It marked Bailey's 100th day since she was born. It was a huge milestone for her and our family. She has been making tremendous progress, especially on the CPAP of 7. We were told that tomorrow morning she will undergo blood work and, depending on the results, she might be weaned down to a CPAP of 6. This brought us one step closer to bringing her home with us. According to her nurses, she had a great weekend and was doing well overall. I couldn't help but ask Bobby when he thought Bailey would finally come home. He hesitated to answer, not wanting to get his hopes up. I could understand his hesitation but also felt excited at the thought of having her home with us soon. So, I predicted that she would come home on July 20th, which was just 20 days away.

Tomorrow, I plan on starting to organize her coming-home party and scheduling her newborn pictures. These thoughts filled my mind as we prepared for another day at the hospital.

Day 101: July 1

I rushed to the hospital with a sense of urgency this morning. Bailey's night nurse had left me a concerning message—they had increased her FIO2 from 32% to 40%, a jump that seemed drastic compared to her levels over the weekend. As I arrived and spoke to the nurse, she couldn't provide an explanation for the sudden change. Upon entering Bailey's room, my heart clenched at the sight before me. Her cannulas were out of her nose. I don't know how long she had the cannulas out of her nose, but that explained the increased need for oxygen. This was not how I wanted to start our day.

I knew from previous experiences that each nurse has their own way of caring for patients, but as a parent, it's important to advocate for your child. Luckily, Deysi was back on day shift today. With her familiar and attentive care, I hoped our day would go smoother.

However, things took a turn for the worse later in the day. Bailey's oxygen and heart rate dropped suddenly, and her lips and body turned blue. My heart raced with fear as she began to vomit after just 15 minutes of feeding. The medical team rushed into the room, frantically suctioning her and using a bag to help regulate her levels. It felt like an eternity, but eventually her vitals stabilized. The doctors suspected she may have aspirated.

After the event, Bailey underwent an X-ray and blood work. Thankfully, her blood work came back normal, but her X-ray showed some abnormalities. Another X-ray was scheduled for the following morning.

I was so shaken by the experience that I didn't want to leave Bailey's side. I made the decision to stay overnight with her in the hospital room. The doctor on call had warned us that another event could occur within the next 12–24 hours if she had indeed aspirated. With Bobby by my side, we made makeshift beds out of chairs and attempted to get some rest.

Thankfully, Bailey had a relatively calm night. She slept on her belly and had no major drops in her vitals. We could finally breathe a sigh of relief—for now.

Day 102: July 1

The night passed quickly; I woke up feeling exhausted. Daysi woke me. She was surprised to see us here. We usually don't stay overnight; that was a first for us. During rounds, the doctor for the day stated that the X-ray didn't show any signs that she had aspirated; he believed she might have just choked. No changes were made to her treatment plan, with the medical team opting to keep a close eye on her condition.

It was bath night for Bailey, and it looked like she truly enjoyed her bath, her smile really does make everyone in the room happy. That girl is going to be something special. During the day Bailey was okay, she seemed to swing a lot, nothing to major, but she we did have to increase her FI02 to 48%. We stayed at the hospital until her nighttime nurse arrived, and I felt comfortable enough to leave. She seemed like a kind and capable caregiver.

Day 103: July 3

Today was a good day. I spent the morning at the hospital before heading home to wash some of Bailey's clothes. While there, painters came to work on her nursery, and it turned out beautifully. I couldn't wait to see the finished project. After finishing up at home, I returned to the hospital, where my parents were waiting.

No changes were made to Bailey's treatment plan during rounds. However, if her X-ray comes back clear tomorrow, they might make some adjustments to her CPAP settings, though those changes wouldn't be implemented until Monday at the earliest.

CHAPTER TEN

Day 104: July 4

T oday was the 104th day of our stay in the hospital, a date that seemed to blur together with all the other holidays we had spent here—Easter, Memorial Day, Mother's Day, Father's Day, and now Fourth of July. Five holidays, each one marked by the sterile walls of this place. I pray that this will be our last holiday in the hospital, but I've learned to make the best of it. Bailey is dressed in her festive Fourth-of-July outfit, bringing a bright spot to an otherwise dreary day.

The hospital organized a firework viewing party in the healing gardens. The bursts of color and light illuminated the dark sky, creating a beautiful display. But Bobby and I were not in the mood to fully appreciate it. Exhaustion and stress had taken its toll on us, causing bickering and tension between us.

Just when I thought the evening couldn't get any better, Amanda joined us outside to watch the fireworks. She shared with us the news that she would be going home sometime this weekend. While I was happy for her, I couldn't help but feel a pang of envy. It reminded me that they don't give you much warning before discharging you from here—just 48 hours' notice, at most.

Day 105: July 5

I want to scream! We were taking a step back, but even as I felt this way, I couldn't be too angry. The doctors' decisions made sense—they wanted to be sure that there was no extra fluid in Bailey's lungs after her accident last Monday. So now we were back at CPAP level 8, giving her lungs more room to expand. They had also started her on diuretics, hoping to release any excess fluid. They planned to keep her on CPAP 8 for the weekend and see how she progressed.

Moreover, in addition to stress with Bailey's health, my boss had scheduled a meeting for Monday to discuss giving me back some of my previous responsibilities. Part of me didn't feel ready to take on more tasks at work while balancing everything with Bailey's care. But, then again, not having much to do at work had allowed me to focus fully on Bailey. Perhaps adding more tasks would be a welcome distraction. As changes continued to come faster than I could process them, I reminded myself not to question it and trust that God wouldn't give me more than I could handle. So, I stayed positive and tried my best to continue being happy and helping others.

With Amanda potentially leaving soon, I wanted to make sure she had something for her son, Niles. So, I took a trip to Carters and Target to get some baby essentials I thought she might need.

May also stopped by the hospital today, and I got the chance to see her as well. Her daughter had undergone a minor surgery, so we caught up and shared some new insights about each other. With our shared last name and similar appearance between my grandfather and her father, we couldn't help but wonder if we were somehow related. And just like for Amanda, I had picked out a small gift for May daughter too. Sidenote: One of my love languages is gift-giving. I find joy in finding meaningful gifts for others to show them how much they mean to me.

Day 106: July 6

Today was a bittersweet day for me. It marked my original due date, the day I had been anticipating for months. To take care of myself, I spent the day away from the hospital, indulging in a much-needed "Me Day." I treated myself to a hair appointment and then met up with my friend Joi and her mother at the mall. As we browsed through shops, I couldn't resist picking out a few things for Bailey's room. After our shopping excursion, we headed back to Joi's house, where we were joined by some friends and enjoyed cooking out on the grill.

Meanwhile, my parents went to spend the day with Bailey at the hospital, which brought me comfort and peace of mind. Even when I couldn't physically be there, knowing that someone was taking care of her eased my worries.

During rounds, there were no significant changes made for Bailey clinically. We were staying steady for the time being, with her on CPAP level 7. I didn't think they would make any more adjustments until Thursday after rounds, assuming her gas levels remained stable. I predicted that they would move her down to CPAP level 6.

Day 107: July 7

I woke up feeling refreshed and ready to enjoy the beautiful weather outside. After visiting Bailey in the morning, I headed out with my friends Joi and Kenya to run some errands and grab lunch. The laughter and good company made for a rejuvenating day. By mid-afternoon, I had returned to the hospital.

Today we went back to the CPAP of 7. I think we are going to keep steady for a few days. My guess is that they won't make any more changes until Thursday after rounds. If her gas is good. I think they will move her to CPAP of 6.

Amanda and her son went home today. They had spent a total of 137 days in the NICU. As I happened to be passing through the hallway, I ran into them just as they were leaving. We took photos together and said our goodbyes before they left for home. The hospital gave him a tiny graduation cap, and I couldn't stop smiling.

I received a text from Amanda later that day, letting me know they had safely arrived home. It was heartwarming to have been able to share in their special moment. This experience filled me with excitement and anticipation for the day when Bailey would also be able to come home with us.

Day 108: July 8

Today was a slow and steady day, much like Bailey's progress. As the hours ticked by, I couldn't help but feel like it was dragging on, as I was trying to get back into the swing of working again. My mind was filled with a list of tasks waiting for me, but I couldn't seem to find the motivation to start on them. Even though there was a possibility that Bailey could be coming home soon, it still felt like a long road ahead.

I knew I'd miss Amanda's presence here—she was someone who truly understood what I was going through. We shared our fears and hopes for our little ones in the NICU. But now there's a new family next door, and I can see that their journey will be just as challenging. They seem like a nice couple, and their baby is even younger than Bailey, still confined to an incubator.

One of the things that kept me going during this time was the amazing nurses who cared for Bailey. Her two primary nurses formed a special bond with her, and it always brought me comfort knowing she was in good hands when I had to leave for a bit.

Day 109: July 9

As I walked into the NICU today, I saw Bailey hooked up to her machines at 30% FIO2. The doctors informed me that she had experienced some events and required an increase in oxygen, but they were able to bring her back down to 30%. This consistency at 30% is progress compared to the past week, when we averaged 34–36%.

My mom came to spend the day with Bailey so I could go home and take care of some household tasks and catch up on TV shows. Before I left, I stopped to introduce myself to the couple two doors down from Bailey's room. Their son was also in the NICU. She was having some placenta and blood pressure issues, and they wanted to deliver the baby as soon as possible. She was due August 22nd and had him over the 4th-of-July weekend.

Their town did not have a level-4 NICU—they only had a level 2—so after she delivered, they were transferred here, to Children's. I learned that they were staying at the local Ronald McDonald house, and they had another son who was staying with their grandparents.

They were about two hours away from home. I could only imagine how difficult this must have been for them.

Day 110: July 10

It's been a staggering 110 days since Bailey entered the world. But she has been thriving and is now clocking in at a healthy 2.27 kilograms, finally reaching the coveted "5-pound club." It's incredible to see how much she has grown from her tiny 1.9-oz frame. I can't wait for the day when I can bring her home.

But as much as I long for that day, I have to ask myself if I am truly ready for it. The truth is, our house is still in disarray and not at all prepared for a baby.

Despite my growing impatience, there were no changes made during rounds today. They did slightly increase her feeds, which is progress. My hope is that her blood work will show improvement tonight, and they might consider moving her down to a CPAP of 6.

Day 111: July 11

I could not sleep last night. I awoke at around 3:00 a.m. and had been up ever since then. I'd been feeling anxious lately and wasn't sure if it was because I had so many tasks on my mind that I wanted to complete, and that I was uncertain where to start or which task to prioritize first. Since I couldn't sleep, I decided to shower and head to the hospital. I quietly slipped out of bed, careful not to wake Bobby, and headed for the shower. The warm water provided a moment of solace, washing away some of the night's anxiety along with my exhaustion.

Dressed and somewhat refreshed, I made my way to the hospital much earlier than usual, arriving at 6:30 a.m. The NICU floor was quieter at this hour, the usual bustle of the day shift not yet in full swing. The nighttime staff were still on, and the daytime staff didn't arrive until at 7:30 a.m. As I approached Bailey's room, to my relief, Bailey's oxygen levels were holding steady at 30%. It might seem like a small thing to some, but in the NICU, these small victories are what we cling to. Each stable day is a step forward, no matter how tiny that step might be. However, my momentary elation was tempered when I learned that her blood work showed higher numbers than the last time. It was a stark reminder that progress in the NICU is rarely linear.

Rosa, Bailey's nurse for the morning shift, greeted me with a kind smile. She must have sensed my disappointment because she gently placed a hand on my shoulder and said, "We just need her to sleep and grow." Those simple words were both a comfort and a challenge. They reminded me that healing takes time, especially for our tiny fighters.

As I settled into the familiar routine of our NICU day, I found myself struggling with impatience. Every fiber of my being wanted to fast-forward to the day when we could finally bring Bailey home. I longed for the moment when the beeping monitors and sterile hospital environment would be replaced by the warm, loving atmosphere of our home.

But I knew that wishing away these days wouldn't help Bailey. What she needed now was for me to be present, to be her advocate, and to celebrate every small step forward. So, I took a deep breath and refocused my energy on the here and now.

I spent the morning talking softly to Bailey, reading her favorite book for the hundredth time. At least, I like to think it was one of her favorite book, because it's one of my favorite childhood books.

As the day shift fully took over, and the NICU came to life around us, I reflected on the long night and early morning. Yes, it had been challenging, filled with worry and restlessness, but it had also brought moments of peace, connection, and small victories.

I realized that this is what our NICU journey is all about: finding strength in the difficult moments, celebrating the tiny triumphs, and always, always moving forward with hope and love for our little fighter. As hard as it is to remain patient, I know deep down that all we can do right now is prepare for the day when Bailey can finally come home with us and cherish every moment of her incredible journey along the way.

Day 112: July 12

I couldn't help but feel that today was going to be special. Arriving at the NICU, I was greeted by MG, Bailey's nurse for the day. Her calm demeanor and gentle smile always put me at ease, and today was no exception.

I had packed a bag full of fresh clothes for Bailey, excited about the prospect of dressing her in a new outfit after her bath. As I carefully laid out the tiny onesie and socks, I marveled at how far we'd come. Just weeks ago, these clothes would have been too big, but now they seemed like they might actually fit. MG, Daysi, and I loved dressing Bailey. We looked forward to bath day, which was a few times a week. I always made sure she had a cute headband to match her outfit, as well as matching sheets. I knew she didn't have a favorite color yet, but she always looked so beautiful in lavender.

MG and I worked together to give Bailey her bath. I loved these moments, feeling like a "normal" mom doing something as simple as bathing my baby. The warm water seemed to soothe Bailey, and I treasured her content little coos while we gently washed her delicate skin.

After the bath, I spent hours by Bailey's side, alternating between watching her peaceful sleep and meticulously planning our family fun day for tomorrow. It was bittersweet—exciting to plan something for my family, but hard to know I'd be away from Bailey. I was grateful for Bobby's offer to stay with her, allowing me this time spend with my family.

As I jotted down ideas for activities and places to visit, I daydreamed about future family outings that would include Bailey. It felt good to allow myself these moments of hope and anticipation.

During rounds, my heart leapt when the doctors mentioned the possibility of lowering Bailey's CPAP to 6 if the weekend went well. It was another small step, but in the NICU, every step forward is a victory to be celebrated.

As the day wound down, I felt a deep sense of contentment. It had been a good day—peaceful, productive, and full of small joys. Leaving the NICU that evening, I turned back for one last look at my brave little girl. "Sweet dreams, my love," I whispered. "Mommy will be back soon." With a heart full of love and hope, I headed home, ready to embrace whatever the next day would bring.

Day 113: July 13

I awoke early, my heart filled with a mix of excitement and guilt. Today I was spending a full day away from the NICU; we were taking a family trip to Lancaster, PA. As we piled into the car, I reminded myself that self-care and family bonding were crucial for our well-being.

Our day was filled with simple joys and new experiences. We made ice cream at the Turkey Hill Ice Cream factory and took a horse-and-buggy ride through the picturesque countryside. We had lunch at a farm-to-table restaurant, followed by a vintage train ride, through scenic Lancaster County.

After spending the morning and early afternoon in Lancaster, we drove to Hershey, PA, to spend the rest of the day at Hershey Park. At Hershey Park, we rode roller coasters and indulged in chocolate treats. Watching other children's play without worry brought tears to my eyes, all I kept thinking about was "will Bailiey get to experience this one day"?. Throughout the day, we received updates about Bailey, each positive report allowing us to relax a little more.

As we drove to the hotel, exhausted but happy, I reflected on the importance of these moments of normalcy. Our lives had been forever changed by our NICU experience, but this day reminded me that joy and family memories were still possible—and necessary. We returned home rejuvenated, better equipped to face the challenges ahead, carrying with us the warmth of a day filled with laughter, love, and simple pleasures.

Day 114: July 14

We packed up and headed back home once everyone awoke. Though I had planned to go straight to the hospital upon our return, time slipped away from us, and we ended up leaving later than intended. Yet, there was still more on my to-do list, including a birthday cookout event that Bobby and I were invited to attend. After stopping by Joi's house to cook with her and catch up on life, we made our way to the birthday celebration, where we spent quality time with friends and indulged in delicious food.

Day 115: July 15

I hadn't seen Bailey in two days, and she looked so much bigger than I remembered. She was growing so much, and I loved it. During rounds this morning, I was a little disappointed. I thought they were going to wean her CPAP down to 6, but they decided not to. They were going to stop the continuous feeds and run the feeds for over two hours. She had been on constant feeds for two weeks, so we were going back to where we left off before her last major event. I believed the goal would be to get her back to running the feeds for an hour to an hour and a half. I needed to find out what the feeding goal was.

Today was picture day in the NICU, and the theme was Olympics. The sight of all the little fighters dressed up in their Olympic-themed costumes brought a smile to my face.

Day 116: July 16

Day 116 dawned like any other in the NICU, but Tuesdays always held a special significance, because these were the days when multiple specialists would converge to check on Bailey, making it both an exciting and anxiety-inducing experience for us parents.

The day began early, with the usual routine of checking Bailey's vitals and speaking with the night nurse for updates. As always, I arrived at the hospital just as the sun was rising, eager to see my little girl and brace myself for the busy day ahead.

By midmorning, the parade of doctors began. First up was the neonatologist, who meticulously reviewed Bailey's progress over the past week. They discussed her respiratory status, noting small but significant improvements in her oxygen requirements. Each percentage point decrease felt like a monumental victory.

Next came the respiratory therapist, who spent time adjusting Bailey's settings and explaining the intricacies of her breathing support. They patiently answered my questions about weaning protocols and long-term respiratory outcomes, their expertise both reassuring and sobering.

The nutritionist's visit was particularly enlightening. We discussed Bailey's feeding plan. Every gram gained was celebrated, proof of her strength and the effectiveness of her care plan.

Perhaps the most anticipated visit was from the developmental specialist. They observed Bailey's responses and movements, providing insights into her neurological progress. Watching them interact with Bailey, encouraging her to track objects and respond to stimuli, filled me with a mixture of pride and hope for her future.

Throughout the day, I constantly took notes, jotting down medical terms to research later and questions to ask at our next care conference. The sheer volume of information was overwhelming, but I was determined to stay informed and involved in every aspect of Bailey's care.

Between doctor visits, I cherished the quiet moments with Bailey. I read to her, sang soft lullabies, and simply held her hand, marveling at how something so small could encompass my entire world. These intimate moments provided a much-needed respite from the clinical discussions and medical jargon that dominated the day.

As evening approached and the flurry of specialist visits subsided, I reflected on the day. The wealth of expertise focused on Bailey's care was both impressive and humbling. Each professional brought a unique perspective to her treatment, all working in concert to give her the best possible chance at a healthy future.

While these busy Tuesdays were emotionally and mentally exhausting, they also filled me with immense gratitude. The dedication of the medical team, the advancements in neonatal care that were giving Bailey a fighting chance, and the small but steady improvements we were seeing all combined to reinforce my hope and determination.

Day 117: July 17

Today brought an unexpected challenge: Bailey's first hearing test. The day began with a mix of anticipation and nervousness as we prepared for this important milestone. The audiologist arrived in the late morning, equipment in tow, ready to assess Bailey's auditory responses.

As the test progressed, I watched intently, trying to decipher the audiologist's expressions. The process seemed to take forever, each moment stretching out as I held my breath, hoping for positive results. When the test concluded, the audiologist's face told me something wasn't right before she even spoke.

The news hit hard: Bailey had failed the hearing test in her left ear. The right ear showed normal responses, but the left ear's results were concerning. The audiologist explained that this doesn't necessarily mean permanent hearing loss, as many factors can influence these early tests in the NICU environment.

We discussed the next steps: A retest would be scheduled in a few weeks, allowing time for any temporary factors to resolve. If the results persisted, a more comprehensive Auditory Brainstem Response (ABR) test would be conducted for a detailed assessment of Bailey's hearing function.

The rest of the day was a rollercoaster of emotions. I found myself oscillating between worry about potential long-term implications and hope that this was just another temporary hurdle. I spent hours researching hearing development in preemies, learning about various types of hearing loss and intervention strategies.

As evening approached, I sat by Bailey's crib, gently stroking her hand. I sang to her softly, wondering if she could hear me clearly, and promising that we would face this challenge together, just as we had faced every other obstacle in her young life.

Before leaving for the night, I spoke with Bailey's primary nurse about the test results. Her reassuring words reminded me that this was just one test, one day in our long journey. She encouraged me to focus on Bailey's overall progress and the many hurdles she had already overcome.

As I headed home, my mind was already planning for the weeks ahead—questions to ask at our next care conference, preparations for the retest, and potential early-intervention options to explore. Despite the setback, I felt a familiar determination rising within me. Whatever the future held for Bailey's hearing, we would face it head-on, armed with knowledge, support, and our usual loving, steadfast commitment to giving her the best possible care.

Day 118: July 18

Today, we experienced a significant milestone in Bailey's care. The day began with a visit from the Bronchopulmonary Dysplasia (BPD) team, who carefully evaluated Bailey's progress. After thorough consideration, they recommended a chest X-ray to get a clearer picture of her lung development. This decision was both exciting and nerve-wracking, as it could potentially reveal important information about Bailey's respiratory status.

The team also suggested increasing Bailey's diuretics, a change aimed at reducing any excess fluid in her lungs that might be hindering her breathing. This adjustment in medication highlighted the delicate balance of treatments required in managing BPD.

Another important development was the decision to transition Bailey from her preemie formula to a more nutrient-dense option better suited for her growing needs. This change signified her progress and the need to support her increasing nutritional requirements as she continued to develop.

The most thrilling news of the day came when we learned that after three challenging weeks on a CPAP setting of 7, Bailey's respiratory support could be reduced to a CPAP of 6. This reduction, though seemingly small, represented a significant improvement in her ability to breathe more independently. It was a moment of triumph that brought tears to our eyes, a tangible sign of Bailey's growing strength.

While it was difficult to predict the exact timeline for further respiratory improvements, I estimated that we might need to stay on this new setting for at least a week or two. This cautious optimism was balanced with the understanding that each baby progresses at their own pace in the NICU.

While I sat by Bailey's bedside, watching her breathe more comfortably with the reduced support, I was filled with a profound sense of hope and pride. I reflected on how far we had come since those early, uncertain days in the NICU. The thought of potentially seeing Bailey breathe entirely on her own in the future, without the assistance of any machines, seemed more real than ever before.

This day marked a turning point, reinforcing our belief in Bailey's resilience and the power of advanced medical care. It also served as a reminder of the importance of patience and perseverance in the face of the many challenges that come with having a premature baby with BPD.

CHAPTER ELEVEN

Day 119: July 19

Bobby and I went to dinner at one of my favorite restaurants, Uncle Julio's. We always order*ed* the same thing: shrimp and steak fajitas, table-side guacamole, and a margarita. I love Mexican food! It *wa*s comforting during this process to still *be* able to enjoy things that *brought us* happiness. After dinner, we went back to our home, *and* lying in our bed felt so good. We d*idn't* come home often, so lying in our own bed felt like a luxury.

I want*ed* to get back to everyday life as quickly as possible, but I knew it *wouldn't* work that way. *I was so* happy that Bailey *was* progressing, so I *knew she was coming* home sooner than later.

Day 120: July 20

I didn't go to the hospital today. In fact, the last few Saturdays, I have not been at the hospital. This is one day a week where I do something fun for myself or work on something to prepare for Bailey's arrival at home.

My sister and I went to the movies, and I saw the remake of one of my favorite childhood movies, *Twister*. The remake was good, but it couldn't compare to the nostalgic feeling of watching a classic '90s movie. The hospital called while I was in the movie theater and scared me half to death. But nothing was wrong with Bailey; they said she was doing great. They just wanted to give me an update on the plan of action because I had missed rounds. They started Bailey on Lasix for the next three days. The Lasix was expected help some more with draining the extra fluid from her lungs. She had an FiO2 of about 33–34% today They mentioned possibly putting her on CPAP of 5 on Monday, and starting to introduce oral feeds sometime next week.

Despite all that was going on, I had managed to finish 80% of Bailey's nursery. There were still some final touches needed—hanging curtains, blinds, mirrors, and pictures and assembling her bookshelf and changing table/dresser—but it was coming together beautifully. As I gazed around the room, imagining my precious daughter finally home with us, my heart swelled with joy and anticipation.

Day 121: July 21

I walked into the hospital earlier than usual, my heart heavy with apprehension. The previous night's nurse had left me unsettled and anxious, so I was eager to see Bailey and get an update on her condition. My experience with nurses during this process varied greatly—some showed great care and compassion while others were cold and detached.

When I asked about Bailey's night, the nurse simply stated that she had experienced desaturation episodes. She provided no further details or explanation. Her nonchalant attitude and lack of engagement left me feeling uncomfortable and uneasy. I knew I didn't want her as Bailey's nurse anymore. Despite Bailey's progress, I couldn't shake the constant fear and worry that consumed me.

Bailey seemed agitated today, refusing her pacifier and looking exhausted and sweaty. I prayed she wasn't getting sick, but her appearance was concerning and not like her usual self. When Bobby got off work today and came to the hospital, he asked if we could leave for a few hours and come back.

To know my husband, you must understand his love for real estate. Bobby loves looking at properties and potential investments. It's one of his favorite pastimes. So when he asked me to go with him to take a ride to look at a house, it wasn't a surprise. During the past few months, Bobby hadn't asked me for much, so if riding around looking at houses was his ideal date, I didn't mind. Of course, I liked the house we went to look at! But buying a new one was the last thing on my mind. Nonetheless, it was fun looking at the house and deciding which room would be the nursery for Bailey if we were to move here.

Bailey also threw up twice today, but what gave me a glimmer of hope was that her heart rate remained stable during the second episode. As a parent of a preemie, learning of any progress in their reflexes feels like a small victory.

Day 122: July 22

Today brought both good news and some concerns for Bailey's health. After seeing elevated blood work levels and a CO_2 reading of 60 (normally low 50s), the medical team decided to extend her Lasix treatment from three to five days. They also switched back to continuous feeds instead of bolus feeding. Additionally, her heart rate was higher than usual, and her white blood cell count was slightly elevated.

Thankfully, all other blood work showed positive results, and there were no signs of infection brewing in Bailey's tiny body. The slight spike in her white blood cells was lower than her normal levels, and her infection marker came back low—a small sigh of relief for us.

Feeling emotionally drained, I decided to go home this afternoon. As much as I needed to be with Bailey, I also needed a break from the constant stress and worry. The feelings of thinking she was getting closer to coming home and something would happen and put us a step back—it was exhausting. I knew it was always a temporary step back, but man could it hurt. I grabbed some lunch on my way home and then crawled into bed in my pajamas and turned on the TV to relax. The tension in my back from the past few days of emotional strain had become nearly unbearable.

Day 123: July 23

I stayed home today and decided to head to the hospital later in the afternoon. I had a lot of work meetings and projects to attend to. It was hard to concentrate on work at the hospital, with all the beeping of the machines and interruptions from the nurses. Working and taking care of Bailey at the hospital started to feel like an impossible task. But I was grateful that my mom and Bobby stayed with Bailey at the hospital so that I could focus on work. The medical team made no changes to her respiratory treatment but did mention conducting a thyroid panel to check for any abnormalities that could be contributing to her increased heart rate. They also discussed giving her the routine four-month vaccines soon, another reminder that our preemie was growing and reaching milestones despite the challenges she was facing every day.

Day 124: July 24

A sense of calmness washed over me when I walked into the hospital room. It was an odd feeling, as the past few days had been filled with anxiety and worry. But today, there was a glimmer of hope that things might finally be looking up.

For the next five days, we would be without our two primary nurses. It was a relief to know that they would be back on duty come Monday, providing a sense of familiarity and comfort. Until then, it seemed like we would have a revolving door of nurses, each new face bringing uncertainty and unease.

No changes were made to Bailey's treatment plan during rounds. All of her blood work and thyroid panel came back normal, which was a huge relief. The doctors speculated that the Lasix she had been taking might have been responsible for her elevated heart rate. Luckily, today was her last day on the medication, and we could expect to see her heart rate return to normal tomorrow.

Bobby is planning to attend a wedding out of town in the coming days, giving him a much-needed break from the stress of staying at the hospital. While I was happy for him, I couldn't help but feel a twinge of nervousness about being alone with Bailey and not having her trusted primary nurses by her side. On top of that, my period finally returned, adding another layer of complication to an already challenging situation. These next few days were going to be quite interesting, to say the least.

Day 125: July 25

I felt a sense of hope today. It wasn't like yesterday, when I didn't feel any hope and just couldn't see the end of the tunnel, struggling to imagine a future when things might be better. But after speaking with the NP this morning and hearing her expert opinion on our next steps, I finally felt a sense of relief. We tried Lasix for five days, but it didn't seem to have any effect. Our current diuretic didn't seem to be helping much either, though it at least kept her steady and consistent. Now, it was time to make some moves. The NP suggested starting a course of steroids in hopes of pushing Bailey over this stubborn hump of no new movement. And if these steroids didn't work, there was always the option of trying D.A.R.T steroids, which had been successful in the past for Bailey. I was hopeful that within the next week, we would finally see progress and be able to reduce Bailey's oxygen requirement.

I walked two rooms down to see if Alysia wanted to grab lunch in the cafeteria. I figured she could use a break as well. During lunch, she shared her traumatic birthing story with me, and I felt grateful for the chance to connect with someone who truly understood what I went through. Alysia's son was going to need surgery soon to remove a piece of his lungs that was causing complications. My heart went out to them, and I prayed everything would go well.

On a positive note, today marked a big milestone for Bailey: She got to sit in her swinger for a few hours! There were a few desaturations, but I believe they were due to feeding issues rather than discomfort. And as if that weren't enough good news, Bailey also made the news today! The NICU photographer took Olympic-themed photos of all the babies last week, and they were featured on the news. It was the cutest thing I've ever seen, and it's moments like these that make it easier for me to be here. Overall, I would say today was a good day.

Day 126: July 26

MG was her nurse today. I always felt at ease when her primary nurses were there. Today was also my mother's birthday, so I planned on leaving early to find her a gift. And yup, I was going to the Hallmark store.

Also, I had everything in my shopping cart to complete Bailey's room. I planned to go over the list with Bobby, as he wanted to feel included in things like decorating her room and picking out furniture. Sometimes I forget that dads get excited about things like this, too!

Bailey's condition saw improvement in the previous 24 hours thanks to the steroids. During rounds, they discussed potentially transitioning her to CPAP of 6 on Monday, pending the results of another blood test on Sunday. I held on to hope and prayed that this plan would come to fruition.

Day 127: July 27

Today brought even more joy as we celebrated my mother's birthday together. We started the morning off with a delicious breakfast in picturesque Georgetown, followed by a round of miniature golf and indulging in ice cream treats. Our family then headed off to play pickleball before gathering at a cozy restaurant for dinner. These moments spent away from the confines of the hospital always bring a sense of normalcy and joy to our lives. They remind me of what we are fighting for and motivate me to keep pushing through.

I was grateful for the evening nurse who cared for Bailey tonight. Her wealth of knowledge and experience put us at ease as she gently encouraged Bobby and me to become more involved in Bailey's care. She reminded us that our ultimate goal was to prepare for bringing Bailey home—not just to focus on reducing her FIO2 levels but also to master all aspects of caring for her medical needs.

Day 128: June 28

Today, doctors were moving Bailey to a CPAP of 6, after almost a week on CPAP of 7. Bobby and I were unsure if they would make this change today or wait until tomorrow, but it seemed that they decided to go forward while she was still on steroids. A small step, but one that brought us closer to our goal.

Day 129: July 29

Another day, another blood test. And this time, it was good news. Bailey's CO2 output dropped from 63 to 51. The doctors discussed keeping things steady for now, not making any changes just yet. They have debating whether or not to start D.A.R.T steroids, but the nurse practitioner believed we should hold off, and I agreed to hold off until her respiratory support improved.

I have continued to learn so much about Bailey's unique personality. She loves her pacifier, being on her belly, and occasionally sitting in her chair. And we hit a major milestone: Bailey became part of the 6-pound club, weighing in at a healthy 6 lbs., 3 oz. Each day was a new discovery, a new challenge, but also a new reason to feel grateful for this precious little girl in my arms.

Day 130: July 30

Today was another busy Tuesday—an eye exam and BPD Team assessment were on the schedule. After 45 weeks corrected age, Bailey, according to the doctor, was no longer at risk for eye disease. However, being only 43 weeks and 3 days old, she would get a follow-up in 2–3 weeks, just to be safe. The doctor had no concerns about her eyes, explaining that any issues would most likely resolve themselves over time. Despite this good news, they still planned to monitor her progress with regular check-ups.

After meeting with the BPD team, it was decided that Bailey was doing exceptionally well and ready to start weaning off the CPAP machine. Her settings could be lowered all the way down to a CPAP of 5, which was a huge milestone in her recovery. This would also be the lowest setting before transitioning to the Vapotherm machine which delivers heated, humidified air and oxygen at high velocities through a nasal cannula, and offer non-invasive respiratory support vs. the CPAP machine which provide continues positive air pressure (which Bailey is currently on).

Day 131: July 31

With X-rays showing positive results and Bailey maintaining a low FIO2 level on CPAP of 5, it was finally time to make the switch to Vapotherm. It came as a surprise when they announced the change would happen today; Bobby and I were both nervous but trusted in their decision. While there wasn't much difference between CPAP of 5 and Vapotherm 4, we knew it would make Bailey more comfortable.

As preparations began for her transition to Vapotherm, I made plans to spend more time at home during this week, starting on Sunday. It was time to get everything in order for her arrival back home.

CHAPTER TWELVE

Day 132: August 1

B ailey's first bottle! I was unable to witness it as I was on a planned sisters' trip out of town. We left early in the morning, and by the time I arrived in New York, my dad had called to tell me she had successfully taken her first bottle. I couldn't help but feel a mixture of excitement for her milestone and sadness that I couldn't be there to see it myself. This was a huge step forward for Bailey, and I knew she was moving in the right direction. For the next few days, the doctors decided not to make any changes to her feeding routine. However, depending on how her blood work looked tonight, they could make adjustments tomorrow. I expected them to increase her bottle feeds.

Day 133: August 2

Today marked the second successful day of bottle feeding for Bailey. She was receiving two feedings via PO—one during the morning shift and one during the night shift. Meanwhile, I was enjoying my time in NY but could not wait to get home and witness all of the new changes Bailey made!

Day 134: August 3

We were moved to a new room today due to staffing and admission issues. It seemed they needed Bailey's old room for a baby with more critical needs. They mentioned that since Bailey was more stable , she might be moved again as they tended to prioritize babies who were able to move around with fewer supplies. Our new room overlooked the "Healing Gardens" and was a corner room close to the door. While it did provide some isolation, we couldn't see much of what was going on outside. But maybe that was a good thing as it allowed us to focus solely on Bailey's progress. However, I did miss the bustling noise and activity from our previous room. I wondered if she came at the end or beginning of rounds in her new room. I did know that being in a different room changed the order of things, and I was curious to find out what that order would be. Today was a significant day, as well; Bailey has been on Vapotherm for five days now, and we will get an update on her internal progress through a blood test. The doctors also mentioned that when she gets closer to going home, she will move to the other side of the NICU, known as the more stable side.

Day 135: August 4

We officially passed Amanda's NICU stay time. Amanda and her son were in the NICU for 134 days, and we were now on day 135.

Day 136: August 5

The hospital was my only destination for the day, with only Bailey by my side. Bobby worked long hours this week, leaving me to handle everything on my own.

During the morning rounds, the doctors decided not to make any changes to Bailey's respiratory treatment, but they did increase her feeds. It was a small victory, but I clung to it as a glimmer of hope.

As evening approached and the sun slowly set outside, I finally left the hospital around 5:30 p.m. Exhausted and hungry, all I had managed to consume was a cup of coffee. It dawned on me that I needed to start taking care of myself too, in order to have enough energy to keep going through these long days in the hospital with Bailey.

Day 137: August 6

I know I have said this a few times, but we were getting closer to the end of this season. I stayed home to get some much-needed rest and to work on my "Operation Bring Bailey Home" list. When I called to see how rounds went, I was informed that tomorrow they were going to move her to Vapotherm setting of 3! That is the last setting of the Vapotherm. The BPD team also said that her lungs sounded good.

Day 138: August 7

My heart swelled with anticipation as we prepared for Bailey's move to Vapotherm setting of 3 today. In addition, her feeds were being increased to 60 ml per feeding, an encouraging sign of progress. Although it was still only two bottles a day—one in the morning and one in the evening—we were finally able to let Bailey determine how much she wanted to eat, just like a typical newborn.

But the most exciting news came when we were told we were moving to the other side of the NICU, the part reserved for babies who were close to going home. I had dreamt of this moment for months, but never thought it would come so soon. As we settled into our new room, I couldn't help but admire its spaciousness and privacy, a luxury we hadn't experienced in our previous cramped quarters. Everyone noted that we had the largest room in the NICU, at the end of hall in the corner, with its own bathroom and shower. Bobby mentioned how useful this room would have been two months ago, and I could only agree. But now, in this moment, I was just grateful for the newfound sense of space and normalcy it provided us with.

Day 139: August 8

It was a beautiful Thursday in August, and I treated myself to a girls' night out. I carefully selected a chic outfit and took my time applying makeup, wanting to look my best for the occasion. We dined at a fancy steakhouse. We ordered appetizers, while I ordered a rib eye steak, and sipped on generous glasses of wine. While we laughed and caught up with one another's lives, The warmth of friendship and good food filled me with nostalgia and contentment.

Day 140: August 9

As the days ticked by, Bailey's nursery took shape. The once-bare walls of the room were now awash in a beautiful coral hue, reminiscent of a perfect, sun-kissed salmon. The soft color seemed to radiate warmth and joy, filling the space with a cozy ambiance. Against one wall stood a unique bookshelf, crafted in the shape of a tree with branches reaching toward the ceiling. Its sturdy wooden shelves held children's books and toys, ready to be read and played with. Coral color lace curtains hung from the windows, allowing just enough light to filter through and cast a peachy glow over the room. In the corner sat a pristine changing table, stocked with all the essentials for taking care of little Bailey. I couldn't wait to hang the custom wooden nameplate that was written in a pretty cursive script. With every detail carefully thought out and lovingly put together, it was clear that this nursery was a labor of love for its soon-to-be occupant.

Day 141: August 10

Yesterday was a difficult day for me as I watched a friend prepare to go into the hospital to deliver her baby at full term, which was something I did not get to experience. I don't know what it's like to pack a hospital bag with all the essentials a new mom needs after giving birth. I don't know what it's like picking out the perfect coming home for your baby. Part of me grieves things like this. As if that weren't enough, I also attended a "Nesting" party for another friend who was expecting. I don't know how to describe this feeling, like you're happy for your friends, and excited for them to enter their new season, but you also feel sorry for yourself because you missed out on things you wanted to experience as a first-time mom. Despite feeling happy for them, a pang of sadness tugged at my heart. The progress that Bailey had made filled me with pride and hope, and I wanted so much for her to come home with us, but I reminded myself to trust in the journey and the timing of it all, knowing that everything would fall into place when it was meant to be.

Day 142: August 11

We just finished rounds this morning. To say I *was* a little disappointed is an understatement. I was hoping that with her doing well with the 90-minute feeds, they would increase the PO bottle feed to 2 bottles a shift, a total of 4 bottles a day. Which means we would be halfway to our feeding goal. I don't know; sometimes I fe*lt* like they are moving too slowly, but I d*idn't* want them to rush. However, I fe*lt* as though we *were* moving much more slowly than usual.

Day 143: August 12

Feeling drained and unwell, I made the decision to stay home today. My body was exhausted from the constant stress and overthinking that came with having a child in the NICU. Each passing moment felt like eternity as I waited for Bailey to come home.

During rounds, I received a call that they were increasing Bailey's bottle feeds to two bottles per shift. This was welcome news as it meant less reliance on her feeding tube. Although I couldn't be there in person, I heard through the phone that the doctor had mentioned weening her off Vaportherm, but the NP intervened and suggested waiting until she mastered bottle-feeding first. They would revisit it on Thursday, taking into account her blood levels. On top of it all, Bailey had officially hit the 7-pound milestone today, a small victory in our quest to bring her home.

Day 144: August 13

I arrived at the hospital in the early morning, my mind already buzzing with all the tasks I needed to accomplish. But as the sun rose higher and the hours passed by, my motivation dwindled and I couldn't bring myself to do any work. It was frustrating, knowing that this was a crucial time for me to be productive, but still, I felt completely stuck.

Despite my lack of productivity, there were happy events happening around me. My friend Kate gave birth today, and I sent her a bouquet of flowers to celebrate. Kenya also received news that her induction date had been scheduled. While I was happy for both of them, it was bittersweet knowing that they would get to take their babies home before I could. But I held on to hope that, soon enough, I would be able to bring my own precious bundle of joy home as well.

Day 145: August 14

This was the slow-and-steady part they don't really prepare you for. You see the finish line, but it still seems so far away. Today during rounds they made no changes, the second day in the row with no changes. This stage of waiting felt like slow motion, each day inching by as we waited for our baby girl to grow stronger and healthier.

But there was one small milestone: The occupational therapists had switched out Bailey's bottle nipple from ultra-preemie to preemie size. It may seem like a small change, but it meant that she could consume more milk in a shorter amount of time. If she did well with this new nipple, then the next steps toward feeding on que.

Day 146: August 15

As my mom and Bobby rushed off to the hospital, my dad and I stayed behind to work on the house. We spent the day assembling Bailey's new changing table/dresser, carefully following the instructions and making sure it was sturdy and safe for our little one. The smell of fresh wood filled the room as we worked, and the steady hum of conversation between us creating a sense of warmth and comfort.

In between furniture building, I took a moment to clean up the dining area. It may not seem like much compared to all the other tasks we have to do, but it felt good to at least have one part of the house in order. Even though there is still so much left to do, I'm proud of what we were able to accomplish today.

Day 147: August 16

A couple days ago, Bobby and I were asked if Bailey could be photographed for the hospital's foundation Holiday campaign. Of course, we said yes. We were also told that the photos would be featured in the *Foundation* magazine and an article about us as well. We were extremely excited and glad to be able to help the hospital in any way possible.

Today was Bailey's photoshoot! She looked absolutely adorable in all of her outfits, and, of course, I snapped a few pictures myself.

Day 148: August 17

A huge milestone today—Bailey took her first whole bottle! At first, she was hesitant and only drank a few milliliters for me. But then her nurse suggested she give it a try, and I gladly agreed. To our surprise, Bailey gulped down the remaining milk in record time—64 milliliters in just 30 minutes! It made my heart swell with pride and joy.

Later that evening, I headed home while Bobby took over the night shift. We've been taking turns caring for Bailey during these past few weeks, which has allowed me some much-needed breaks. It's been wonderful to come home after a long day at the hospital, take a hot shower, and relax with a warm meal before heading back to our little fighter's side.

CHAPTER THIRTEEN

Day 149: August 18

MG was back! I have said over and over: Having primary nurses who know your baby makes a world of difference. It's good for the baby and the parents. I didn't have to worry as much. MG knew Bailey, she cared for Bailey, and I could relax knowing that she was with someone she knew.

There were no changes during rounds today.

Feeling a sense of lightness, I left the hospital briefly to pamper myself with a manicure and pedicure. It had been over a month since I last took time for myself, and it felt like a much-needed break from the constant worry and stress.

Day 150: August 19

During daily rounds, the doctors warned us that this phase would be the most challenging yet. Unlike respiratory issues that could be addressed with various medications and machines, feeding was solely up to Bailey. She would have to take in enough nourishment on her own terms.

The volume of Bailey's feeds had been increased from 64 ml to 68 ml. It seemed like every time Bailey reached a goal, it was quickly pulled a little farther away. But deep down, we knew that the medical team was doing what was best for our little girl.

And today, there was even more progress. Bailey had taken in more than 30 ml of milk by mouth during the daytime bottles—a significant improvement compared to previous days. It may not seem like much to some, but to these anxious parents, it meant everything.

Day 151: August 20

Today, I captured a video of Bailey that I know will become one of my most cherished memories. Her beautiful smile and infectious laughter radiated pure joy and brought warmth to my heart. Every day, seeing her happy and smiling brings me so much comfort.

Day 152: August 21

As the sun sank below the horizon, Bobby and I eagerly prepared for our long-awaited parents' night out. Our friends joined us, and together we made our way to a lively concert. The air was filled with excitement and anticipation as we approached the venue. Once inside, we were swept up in the pulsing beat of the music and surrounded by a sea of swaying bodies. Joy and energy radiated from the stage, drawing us in farther with each passing moment. We danced and sang until our voices were hoarse, lost in the moment and each other's company. This night was a much-needed escape from our busy, very stressful lives, a chance for us to reconnect and let loose. As we made our way home, we were both filled with contentment and gratitude for such a magical date night.

Day 153: August 22

I woke up this morning with a familiar mix of hope and anxiety as I prepared for another day at the NICU. As I walked into Bailey's room, I couldn't help but feel a surge of love and determination. Today was Thursday, August 22nd—Day 153 in the NICU.

I listened intently while the doctors discussed Bailey's progress during rounds. My heart skipped a beat when they announced their decision to make changes to her feeding regimen. They explained that they would be adjusting the volume and increasing her calorie intake, aiming to get her closer to her goal of 80%. I felt a glimmer of hope; this change could be a significant step forward in Bailey's development.

As they discussed the details, I learned that they would be decreasing her feeds from 68 ml to 60 ml. It might seem like a small change to some, but to me, it represented a world of progress. Each milliliter was a step toward bringing Bailey home, and I clung to that thought.

I asked questions, wanting to understand every aspect of this new plan. The doctors patiently explained how the increased calorie intake would support Bailey's growth and development. They reassured me that they would closely monitor her response to these changes.

Throughout the day, I watched as the nurses implemented the new feeding plan. I held Bailey's hand during her feeds, whispering words of encouragement. "You've got this, Bailey boo," I said softly, hoping that, somehow, she could understand how proud I was of her strength.

As evening approached, I reflected on the day's events. This adjustment in Bailey's care plan filled me with renewed hope. It was a reminder that, even after 153 days, progress was still happening. Every small step forward was a victory, and today, we had taken another step on our road home.

Before leaving for the night, I thanked the nurses and doctors for their continued dedication to Bailey's care. As I kissed Bailey good-night, I whispered, "Keep growing strong, my love. We're getting there, one day at a time."

Driving home, I felt a mix of emotions—gratitude for the progress, hope for the future, and an undying love for my resilient little girl. Day 153 had brought us one step closer to our goal, and I was ready to face whatever Day 154 would bring.

Day 154: August 23

The day of peace and resolution had finally arrived, bringing with it a sense of relief and exhaustion. The weight of the journey had taken a toll on my mind, constantly churning with frustration and anger over things I couldn't control. But today, I made the conscious decision to let go of those negative emotions.

As the sun began to set, I made my way to a comfortable chair near the window in Bailey's room.

I took a deep breath and closed my eyes, letting go of all the things I couldn't change and focusing instead on the things within my control. Tonight, I would rest peacefully knowing that I had made the choice to find peace within myself.

Day 155: August 24

On the 155th day, I made the decision to stay a second night in a row at the hospital. I was so determined to get Bailey to finish all her bottles, and it just seemed like Bailed didn't do so well with the night feeds. Despite the discomfort and constant interruptions from her nighttime nurse checking on her, I knew that staying by her side was worth any sacrifice in order to bring her home one day sooner. home with me.

Day 156: August 25

Today was an unexpected whirlwind of events. I awoke to searing pain radiating from my right foot. As Bobby stirred next to me, I knew I needed to get to the doctors quickly. My foot was throbbing and pulsing, making it impossible for me to stand or walk.

I had Bobby take me to the nearest hospital. After what felt like an eternity, a doctor finally came to see me. He grimaced upon seeing my swollen and discolored foot, muttering that the Nurse shave have brought me back sooner. After an x-ray revealed no fractures or breaks, they ran a series of tests to rule out any other potential issues, including a blood clot.

After what seemed like hours of waiting and worrying, the results came back—I had contracted some type of bacterial infection. It was likely that I picked it up from stepping on something during one of my recent visits to the hospital. The doctors instructed me to rest and elevate my foot for a few days, along with taking a strong dose of antibiotics. Now all I could do was hope for the swelling to go down and for the medication to work its magic.

Day 157: August 26

The pain that had wracked my body yesterday had subsided slightly, but it was replaced with an overwhelming fatigue that seemed to weigh me down more than any physical ache ever could. I knew it was probably due to the medication I was prescribed, but that didn't make it any easier to bear.

I spent most of the day in bed, only getting up when necessary to use the bathroom or grab something to eat. It was emotionally taxing not being able to visit Bailey at the hospital because of my own health issues, but I had learned to lean on others for help and support. Today, Bobby took the reins and spent the whole day with her at the hospital, while his parents came in the evening to visit.

Daysi, one of Bailey's nurses, was also on duty today, which brought me some comfort, being stuck at home. During rounds, doctors decided to increase her feedings from 60 to 64 milliliters. They also mentioned that Bailey wasn't taking as much as she used to during her feeds. While some of this decrease could have been due to her actual appetite, I couldn't help but feel that her exhaustion during the day played a big role as well. She had been staying awake through the night lately, making it harder for her to stay alert during the day

Day 158: August 27

This is Day two of not being at the hospital due to my foot injury. Despite missing Bailey, I was grateful for my parents' constant presence and involvement in her life. My mom had taken the first shift while my dad took over later.

I was informed, there were no major changes to report, but the doctors noted that Bailey had consumed 54% of her bottles. It wasn't quite the goal of 80%, but it was still progress.

Later in the day, the BPD team arrived and discussed with us and the primary team about potentially starting Bailey on Lasix. This would help wean her off FIO2 support and help her transition to a wall cannula, using an oxygen tank.

Day 159: August 28

I couldn't shake the feeling that we weren't pushing hard enough for answers and solutions to improve Bailey's feeding intake. In conversations with her occupational therapist and nurse, they expressed that her oxygen requirement should have changed weeks ago—she should have been on a nasal cannula by now. Perhaps this change could also aid in her feeding, as it would reduce the amount of air she needed to work against.

Day 160: August 29

Day two on the Lasix! Today was such a great day! We are FINALLY on nasal cannula. I had pictured this day in my head for so many months. Even though I knew it was going to happen soon, when it happened it felt so unreal. She has been doing great on the Nasal Cannula. She also took every bottle that was offer during day shift, and was still wide awake after each bottle. Which goes to show me that, she is not exhausted or tired after taking her bottle. That less air has helped her take in more. I'm hoping this means she will sleep less during the day.

Day 161: August 30

I spent Bailey's second day on 2 liters of oxygen at home, working on organizing the house and making it more comfortable for her. The kitchen was meticulously cleaned and preparations were made for upcoming additions to keep it organized. Despite still being a work in progress, it was all coming together nicely and would be completed by Sunday. Plans were also made to work on creating a coffee and bottle station and finishing the dining room. A sense of productivity filled the air as each task was tackled with determination and love for my little one.

Day 162: August 31

As the days stretched on, I found myself losing track of time and feeling unsure about when Bailey would finally come home. This feeding struggle seemed never-ending, like a dark tunnel with no light at the end. I had naively thought it would be easy, but after a month we had barely made any progress. Today, I am supposed to attend two baby showers, but the thought of being around others and celebrating their joy only adds to my frustration. It's like I'm stuck in a cycle of anger and confusion. Why are we still here? None of it makes sense to me. The weight of this struggle weighs heavy on my shoulders, making each day feel like an eternity.

Day 163: September 1

This Sunday marked a breakthrough for me. I woke up with a new-found determination to stop complaining and start making things happen. The weight of our impending tasks hung heavily in the air, but I refused to let it crush me any longer. We had been waiting for Bailey to come home for far too long, and I was tired of watching the days slip by without any progress.

Bobby and I sat down for a deep conversation this morning, discussing the importance of giving each other grace in our marriage. Our current situation would test even the strongest of unions, and it was not an easy journey.

The nurse practitioner came to speak with us about next steps and possible options for Bailey's care. Despite her month-long practice with bottle feeding, little progress had been made. It seemed that the medical team was starting to consider alternative options for getting her home, as the only thing keeping her in the hospital was her difficulty with feeding. They presented us with two choices: transferring Bailey to a rehabilitation center focused solely on feeding practice, or moving her to another unit within the hospital for the same purpose. These options were given because, technically, she no longer required intensive care and was no longer considered a critical patient. The final option presented was a surgical procedure involving inserting a G-tube, which would require intubation while she was under anesthesia. None of these choices was ideal, and we felt overwhelmed by the weight of such difficult decisions looming over us.

Chapter Fourteen

Day 164:September 2

Today Bobby and I headed to Virginia to attend his aunt's memorial. It was a bittersweet day, but we were determined to make the most of it. As we walked inside the church, I could feel Bobby's hand tightly gripping mine, reminding me that we were in this together.

Last night, we had stayed up late discussing our options with two different nurse practitioners who knew Bailey's history like the backs of their hands. Their words weighed heavily on our minds.

We both knew that a decision needed to be made soon, but it wasn't an easy one. We had gone back and forth endlessly, weighing the pros and cons, struggling to come to a final conclusion. This was one of the hardest decisions we would ever have to make.

Day 168: September 6

It was Friday, and Bobby and I were hopeful for a breakthrough in Bailey's feeding. To our delight, she took 60% of her feeds today—three full bottles in a row—two with Bobby, and one with me. The room filled with an air of optimism as we realized that Bailey was showing us she could do it. Not wanting to lose the momentum, Bobby and I decided to stay the night at the hospital. We wanted to continue feeding her, even if it meant sacrificing our rest.

Day 169: September 7

The next day brought mixed emotions. While yesterday had been a success with feeding, today we only saw 34% completion. I spent the morning at home, exhausted from staying at the hospital overnight. But, despite my tiredness, I knew I needed to return to the hospital to wash and bring back clean clothes for Bailey. I didn't want Bailey to run out of clean clothes. Though I longed to stay at home and rest, I knew I had to make my way back to the hospital, where Bailey needed me the most.

Day 170: September 8

After spending 169 days on the unit, Bailey was finally getting her term MRI done. This would confirm that her brain was developing properly, a hope we had held onto tightly from the start. It was a momentous occasion, as it marked Bailey's first time leaving the unit since her arrival. The air was filled with anxious anticipation as we awaited the results.

Today, I woke up feeling the need to put my trust back into God. I knew I needed to keep my prayers simple and specific, asking for exactly what I wanted and praying that prayer every day. I even decided to fast as a way to show my dedication.

Day 174: September 12

The next day, I would be leaving for a few days on a girls' trip to New Orleans. When I first booked this trip, I thought Bailey would be home by this time. But with her still in the hospital, I couldn't help but feel nervous about leaving. As I spent the day at the hospital with Bailey, my mind began to drift to thoughts of packing and leaving. It wasn't until around 6 p.m. that I finally left the hospital for some dinner before heading home to pack for our trip. The excitement mixed with apprehension made for an interesting mix of emotions as I prepared for my temporary leave from the unit.

Day 180: September 18

Today was the first day we hit the 70s! Bailey did 71% of her feeds, and I was so freaking proud of her. When we returned to the room after rounds, we said, "Good job, Bailey!" She smiled so hard and started laughing. I never felt so good. I knew she could do it. I had been on the fence the past few days about whether or not we needed to do the surgery or go to the rehabilitation center, but after today's rounds, I think she just needed more time.

Day 181: September 19

Another day, another achievement. This time, Bailey hit 78% of her feeds! Even if this is the highest she reached in terms of progress, I was filled with nothing but pride for her determination and resilience. She showed everyone that she was capable of overcoming any obstacle. After today's rounds, my doubts about needing surgery or going to a rehabilitation center began to fade—it seemed like all she needed was more time to keep pushing forward.

Day 182: September 20

As I walked into the hospital room, my frustration was evident. The nurse on duty last night rushed through feeding Bailey, resulting in her consuming the least amount of food she had in weeks. But perhaps it was a blessing in disguise, forcing me to make a decision about her future care. For the past two weeks, I had been stuck between getting her a G-tube or sending her to a rehabilitation center. Yesterday, I would have chosen the rehab center, but now I'm leaning toward the G-tube.

During rounds, we were told that Bailey consumed 64%, which was better than expected considering she only received two 15 ml feedings during the night shift.

Bailey was officially on 1 liter! This was a big accomplishment for her. I was told yesterday that they send babies home on 1 litter of oxygen.

Day 183: September 21

Yesterday was my sister's 30th birthday, and we celebrated with an adult field day–themed party. It was a welcome break from the stress of being in the hospital, but it can also be difficult when everyone asks about Bailey's condition and when she will come home.

During morning rounds, the medical team discussed their recommendations for Bailey's care and the options of a G-tube or rehabilitation center once again.

Day 184: September 22

Today was a special day. It's Bailey six-month birthday, halfway to one year old, and she had a special reason to celebrate. Bailey had completed 91% of her feed goal yesterday, her highest accomplishment yet. I beamed with pride as I decorated the room with a pink banner that read "6 months" and passed out party hats. I also brought gifts for Bailey to enjoy once she came home. For the first time in six months, we could see the light at the end of the tunnel. During rounds with the medical team, the word "discharge" was finally mentioned, a hopeful sign that we were getting closer to bringing Bailey home.

As if to celebrate this momentous occasion, Bailey took all of her bottles today at 100%, a feat that would have seemed impossible just a few months ago. Every sip brought her closer to reaching her full potential and leaving this sterile hospital environment behind.

As we looked toward the future with optimism and gratitude, I couldn't help but think that this was truly a great day. A day to mark on the calendar as a reminder of how far we had come and how much further we would go together.

Day 185: September 23

Today was one of the happiest days of my life. They removed the NG feeding tube from Bailey's nose and went to adlibs/shift minimum for feeding. My baby girl did it!! They had the case manager come talk to us about ordering the equipment to our home, and scheduling a home visit for her nurse visit, PT, and OT. I was so excited. However, there was still a lot of work to be done. So the next couple of days were going to be hectic, but I was up for the challenge. The goal was to wean her to ½ liter of oxygen on Wednesday. We needed to keep Bailey motivated and keep up eating well.

Day 186: September 24

Bailey had her first day without her feeding tube, and she handled it like a champ. She met her shift minimum. Despite this success, her eye exam didn't bring any significant changes. They were still waiting for eye vessels to "straighten up"; the doctor mentioned that the issue had not resolved itself, but fortunately, it hadn't worsened, either. Bailey needed to have a follow-up appointment at an outpatient clinic in about 2–3 weeks. I was just happy this wasn't something that was going to keep us there, and we can work on this outpatient.

Day 187: September 25

With a renewed determination, my goal for the next few days was to take the time and finish the house. Today, friends and family came over to lend a hand and get things started. I couldn't believe how much work still needed to be done.

Meanwhile, Bobby stayed at the hospital to continue working on feeding with Bailey. He learned that Bailey always finished her bottle if he turned on *Moana*. It became their thing. He swore this movie was helping her drink her bottle more, but hey it seemed to be working! We probably watched this movie 100 times this week.

Day 189: September 27

After two-and-a-half long days of hard work, the house was finally put together. And it looked beautiful. Not since before my pregnancy have I seen my home this organized and polished. The memories of sickness and exhaustion during those 6 months resurfaced, making me realize just how neglected household chores had been. But seeing my house back in order filled me with excitement for the next chapter of my life as a mother.

I took advantage of the time to nest and prepare for Bailey's arrival. Her belongings were neatly arranged, and last-minute items were purchased. The anticipation of her homecoming only grew stronger.

Day 190: September 28

I awoke on Saturday morning, Day 190, my heart racing with a mixture of excitement and nervous anticipation. In just two more days, after what felt like an eternity of 200 days in the hospital, we would finally be bringing Bailey home. The realization hit me in waves throughout the day, each time filling me with an indescribable joy.

After 192 days, Bailey was coming home on a half-liter of oxygen. Although we tried for a few hours of room air, she did not pass the test; she was not ready. She did not require any G-tube or any other surgery before leaving. Although we were coming home with a long list of medications that she would probably be on for the next couple of months, these medications would continue helping with her respiratory support. We were also thankful that our insurance covered weekly home visits from a nurse, as well as weekly visits from OT and PT.

I spent the morning going through Bailey's NICU room, carefully packing up the mementos of our long stay—the milestone cards, the tiny outfits she had outgrown, and the countless cards from well-wishers. Each item held a story, a memory of our roller-coaster journey, and I found myself tearing up when I placed them in boxes.

As I sat in the familiar rocking chair by Bailey's crib, I could only marvel at how far we'd come. I remembered the fear and uncertainty of those first days, when Bailey was so tiny and fragile. Now, as I watched her peacefully sleeping, strong and ready to face the world, I felt an overwhelming sense of pride and love.

The nurses, who had become like family, stopped by throughout the day to share in our excitement and offer last-minute advice. Their support had been invaluable, and I knew I would miss their constant presence and reassurance.

In the afternoon, Bobby and I met with the discharge coordinator to go over final preparations. While we discussed medication schedules, follow-up appointments, and emergency procedures, the reality of taking full responsibility for Bailey's care outside the NICU began to sink in. It was daunting, but I felt ready. We had learned so much during our time here.

Later, while I held Bailey for her evening feed, I whispered to her about all the adventures awaiting us at home. I described her nursery, told her about our family that was eager to meet her, and promised her a lifetime of love and care. The excitement bubbling within me was almost tangible.

Before leaving for the night, I took one last look around the NICU. This place that had been our second home for so long would soon be just a memory. I felt a surprising pang of nostalgia, knowing that despite the challenges, this was where Bailey had grown strong, where we had become parents, and where countless miracles had unfolded.

As I drove home, my mind raced with all the preparations still
to be done. But underlying the to-do lists and nervous energy was
an overwhelming sense of joy and gratitude. In two days, we would
finally be a family under one roof. The long days of separation and
the heartache of leaving the hospital without our baby would soon be
behind us.

I fell asleep that night with a smile on my face, dreaming of the
moment we would walk through our front door, Bailey in our arms,
ready to start our new life together. The countdown to homecoming
had begun, and I could hardly wait for the next chapter of our journey
to unfold.

CHAPTER FIFTEEN

Day 191: September 29

Anticipation built up in my chest like a balloon expanding with each breath. The big day was almost here: Bailey was coming home. After she passed her final test, the car seat test, I knew we were finally in the clear. A sense of relief and excitement washed over me, but a small voice of doubt still lingered in the back of my mind. What if something went wrong? What if she stopped drinking her bottles again or her lab test results came back abnormal? Despite these worries, I couldn't help but feel giddy like a child on Christmas Eve. Tomorrow would be the start of a new chapter, one that I had been waiting for since the moment Bailey entered this world.

Day 192: September 30

Bailey was finally coming home today. The weather was starting to change; it felt like a perfect fall morning. I was emotional realizing we didn't have to spend another season here at the hospital. We spent part of winter, spring, and summer in the hospital. It's so funny to me how life works. I used to walk these hospital floors daily for close to four years for work, and I never imagined I would walk these walls as a mother of a patient.

When we arrived at Bailey's room, I finished packing the remaining items. I never realized how much we had brought here over the last several months. I felt like I was moving my child out of her college dorm.

During morning rounds, an air of anticipation buzzed around us as we confirmed that all medical equipment was delivered and ready to be installed in our home, the faint beeping of monitors a reminder of what lie ahead. We also had to ensure we picked up Bailey's prescriptions from the hospital pharmacy.

Once rounds were completed, a wave of relief washed over us as we received the final go-ahead for Bailey's discharge. We were merely waiting for the discharge papers, our hearts racing with excitement for our family, who couldn't wait to finally meet Bailey. Only her grandparents had had the privilege so far, and the aunts and uncles were practically bouncing with eagerness. The hospital staff shared in our joy, each of them offering bittersweet smiles and hugs, expressing how much they would miss our little girl. The bond formed over the past six months had brought us together in shared struggles and victories, during which they had witnessed my moments of vulnerability—tears streaking my face, my hair a disheveled mess, and days of wearing the same outfit without a second thought.

As the afternoon rolled around, and we were given the official green light to leave, the atmosphere shifted dramatically. While we walked out, Bailey was greeted with a red carpet, the staff and doctors erupting in cheers, their applause ringing in my ears like the triumphant roar of a crowd at a championship game. It felt as if we had just won the Super Bowl, an exhilarating moment filled with joy and a bittersweet farewell.

Chapter Sixteen

The First Thirty Days Home

A whirlwind of emotions swept over me when I walked out of the NICU for the last time. The excitement of finally bringing Bailey home after nearly 200 days was overwhelming, but it was tinged with anxiety and disbelief. Waving goodbye to the NICU staff, who had become like family, I felt a bittersweet pang in my chest. Their cheers of encouragement echoed in my ears as we made our way to the elevator, and I found myself hesitating before pressing the button to leave the 6th floor, our home for the past six-and-a-half months.

The walk to the car was surreal. Each step felt like a milestone, moving us farther from the NICU and closer to our new reality. As we carefully secured Bailey in her car seat, panic started to set in. Were we really ready for this? The whole ride home, I couldn't take my eyes off her, half-expecting to wake up and find myself back in the NICU.

We were fortunate to have our parents follow us home, their presence a comforting reminder that we weren't alone in this new chapter. As we crossed the threshold of our house, I was acutely aware that while we were home, our story was far from over. Bailey still needed oxygen support and a regimen of medications. Our living room had been transformed into a mini-NICU, complete with medical equipment and supplies.

That first night was a mix of joy and terror. Every little sound Bailey made had me rushing to her side. The beeping of her oxygen monitor, once a constant backdrop in the NICU, now seemed deafening in the quiet of our home. Sleep was elusive as we vigilantly watched over our little fighter.

The next day brought our first real test: Bailey's follow-up appointment with her primary care doctor. It was a rainy day, and the simple task of getting to the doctor's office felt like a monumental expedition. Navigating traffic, finding parking, and lugging all of Bailey's oxygen equipment through the rain was exhausting. But as we sat in the waiting room, Bailey calmly nestled in my arms, I felt a surge of pride. We were doing this. We were her parents, out in the real world, advocating for her care.

The first couple of weeks home were a blur of sleepless nights, medication schedules, and constant vigilance. We worked tirelessly to create a routine that accommodated Bailey's needs while trying to establish some semblance of normalcy. Every diaper change, every feeding, every dose of medication felt like a victory, all proof that we could do this.

Our home took on a new character. The living room became command central, with a whiteboard tracking Bailey's feeds, medications, and oxygen levels. Our kitchen counter was a pharmacy of syringes, pill bottles, and feeding supplies. But amidst the medical paraphernalia, there were signs of joy—congratulatory cards, flowers from well-wishers, and the ever-growing collection of "normal" baby items we were finally able to use.

The holidays arrived, bringing a new dimension to our homecoming. Decorating for Christmas with Bailey at home felt miraculous. As we hung ornaments and strung lights, I found myself tearing up, remembering the previous months spent in the NICU, uncertain of what the future held. Now, here we were, celebrating as a family in our own home.

Family visits were both wonderful and stressful. While we cherished introducing Bailey to her extended family, we were also hyper-vigilant about germs and overstimulation. Every visitor was met with hand sanitizer and strict instructions about our "no kissing the baby" rule. It was challenging to balance our desire to celebrate with our need to protect Bailey's fragile health.

As the days passed, we slowly found our rhythm. Bailey's first bath at home, her first smile that wasn't attributed to gas, the first time we ventured out for a short walk—each moment was a celebration. But there were hard times, too. Nights when the oxygen alarms wouldn't stop beeping, days when reflux made feeding a battle, moments of sheer exhaustion when we wondered if we were doing everything right.

Through it all, we leaned on each other and the support system we had built. Video calls with our NICU friends became a lifeline, a reminder that we weren't alone in this post-NICU world. The online support groups I had joined during our NICU stay became even more valuable, offering advice and encouragement as we adjusted to this new normal.

As we approached the one-month mark at home, I started to reflect on how far we'd come. The fear and uncertainty of those first days had given way to a cautious confidence. We were no longer NICU parents; we were simply parents, learning and growing alongside our miraculous daughter.

Looking at Bailey, peacefully sleeping in her crib (finally out of her NICU-style bassinet), I felt a profound sense of gratitude. Bailey has always been a calm baby, not a crier, and sometimes I feel like she acts like she's been in the world before; nothing seems to faze her. Like most babies, she cries when she is hungry, but other than that, she was smooth sailing (at least for now).

The journey had been long and challenging, but here we were, home and together. I gently kissed her forehead and whispered a promise that no matter what challenges lay ahead, we would face them together, our little family of three, stronger for all that we had overcome.

CHAPTER SEVENTEEN

FAMILY PHOTOS

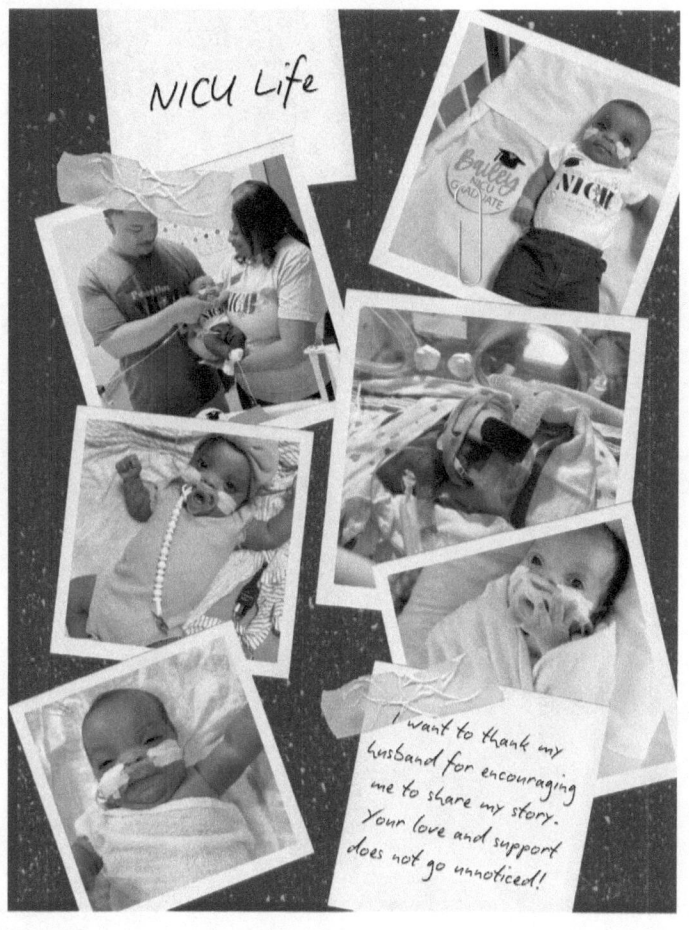

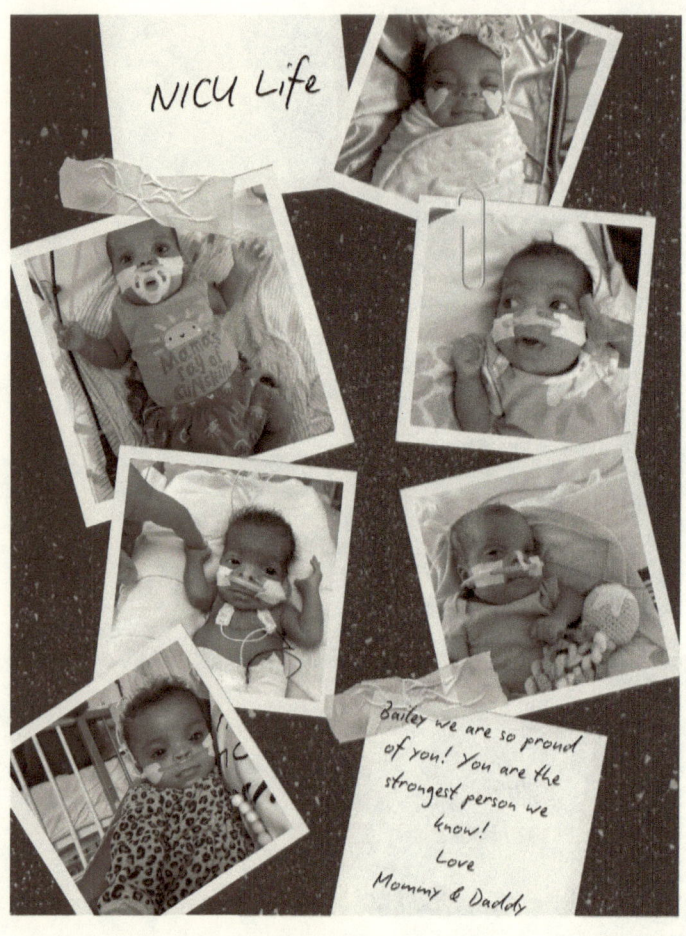

NICU Life

Bailey we are so proud of you! You are the strongest person we know!

Love
Mommy & Daddy

Home &
Thriving

Chapter Eighteen

Part 2: NICU Parents' Guide

As I reflect on my NICU journey, I realize how pivotal this chapter is in bridging my personal experience with the practical guidance I wish I had had during those challenging days. The isolation I felt as a NICU parent was overwhelming, and I remember desperately searching for books that could offer both comfort and practical advice. Unable to find anything that was truly helpful, I turned to journaling on day 68 of our NICU stay.

This practice became my lifeline, a source of strength and perspective. Flipping through past entries helped me recognize our progress and find hope during the darkest times. It was this personal experience of finding solace in writing that inspired me to create this book.

Now, as I introduce Part 2 of this book—a comprehensive parent guide for navigating the NICU—I'm filled with a sense of purpose. While sharing my story offers emotional support and relatability, I recognized the critical need for practical, actionable advice for fellow NICU parents. This guide is the culmination of my experience, countless hours of research, and the invaluable knowledge gained from healthcare professionals throughout our experience.

In the upcoming sections, you'll find guidance on understanding NICU levels, decoding medical terminology, communicating with your medical team, maintaining your mental health, bonding with your baby in the NICU, and preparing for life after discharge. My goal is to empower you with knowledge, helping you become the best advocate for your baby.

I want you to know that while every NICU experience is unique, having a roadmap can provide immense comfort and confidence during this overwhelming time. I encourage you to use the upcoming guide alongside the personal narrative I've shared. It's my sincere hope that by combining my story with practical advice, this book will serve as the comprehensive support system I wish I had had, offering both emotional connection and actionable strategies for navigating the complex world of the NICU.

As we transition from my personal story to this practical guide, I want you to feel prepared and supported. Remember, you're not alone in this journey. Let's take this next step together, arming ourselves with knowledge and hope for the challenging but rewarding path ahead.

CHAPTER NINETEEN

WELCOME TO THE NICU

The Neonatal Intensive Care Unit (NICU) is a specialized hospital department designed to care for premature and critically ill newborns. For many parents, entering the NICU for the first time can be an overwhelming experience. The environment is filled with advanced medical equipment, the constant hum of monitors, and the sight of tiny babies in incubators, all attended to by a dedicated team of medical professionals.

Understanding the NICU environment is crucial for parents, all of whom have whom have suddenly found themselves in this unknown environment. The NICU is more than just a hospital ward; it's a highly specialized unit equipped with state-of-the-art technology and staffed by experts in neonatal care. These units are designed to provide around-the-clock intensive care for newborns who need extra support due to various medical conditions.

Babies may require NICU care for several reasons:

- Premature birth (born before 37 weeks gestation)

- Low birth weight (less than 5.5 pounds)

- Respiratory distress syndrome

- Infections

- Congenital abnormalities

- Complications during delivery

The level of care provided in the NICU is categorized into four distinct levels, each offering increasingly specialized care:

Level I (Well Newborn Nursery)

- Provides care for healthy, full-term newborns capable of neonatal resuscitation at every delivery

- Evaluates and provides postnatal care for stable, term newborns

- Stabilizes and transfers newborns who require a higher level of care

Level II (Special Care Nursery)

- Cares for infants born 32 weeks gestation or later and weighing 1500 grams or more

- Provides care for infants with moderate complications that are expected to resolve rapidly

- Offers mechanical ventilation for brief durations (less than

24 hours) or continuous positive airway pressure

- Can stabilize infants born before 32 weeks gestation until transfer to a higher-level facility

Level III (Neonatal Intensive Care Unit)

- Provides comprehensive care for extremely premature infants (less than 32 weeks gestation) or critically ill newborns of any gestational age

- Offers sustained life support, including prolonged mechanical ventilation

- Provides a full range of respiratory support and advanced imaging services

- Has pediatric surgical specialists available for consultation and procedures

Level IV (Regional NICU)

- Offers the highest level of neonatal care

- Provides care for the most complex and critically ill newborns

- Located within institutions capable of performing surgical repair of complex congenital or acquired conditions

- Maintains a full range of pediatric medical and surgical subspecialists on site

- Facilitates transport and provides outreach education

Personal note: Our personal experience with Bailey's care illustrates the importance of these different levels of care. Bailey was initially cared for in a Level III NICU, which provided advanced care for her premature condition. However, as her needs became more complex, she was transferred to a Level IV NICU at Children's Hospital, where she could receive the highest level of specialized care.

This transfer between different levels of NICUs is not uncommon. As a baby's condition changes, they might be moved to a higher or lower level of care as needed. This ensures that each infant receives the most appropriate care for their specific needs at any given time.

The NICU environment is designed to mimic the womb as much as possible, with controlled temperature and humidity, minimal lighting, and noise-reduction measures. Each baby in the NICU has their own space, often in an incubator or warmer, surrounded by necessary medical equipment.

Key Components of a Typical NICU Setup Include

- Incubators or radiant warmers to maintain body temperature

- Monitors for heart rate, breathing, blood pressure, and oxygen levels

- Ventilators or CPAP machines for breathing support

- Intravenous (IV) lines for medication and nutrition

- Feeding tubes for babies unable to feed orally

The NICU Staff Typically Includes

- Neonatologists (doctors specializing in newborn care)

- Neonatal nurses

- Respiratory therapists

- Nutritionists

- Physical and occupational therapists

- Social workers

- Lactation consultants

These professionals work together as a multidisciplinary team to provide comprehensive care for each baby. For parents, any amount of time in the NICU can be emotionally challenging. It's common to feel a range of emotions, including fear, anxiety, guilt, and helplessness. However, it's important to remember that the NICU staff are not just there for the babies; they're also there to support parents. Many NICUs offer support services for families, including counseling, parent education classes, and support groups.

Understanding the NICU environment, levels of care, and the roles of various healthcare professionals can help parents feel more empowered and involved in their baby's care. While the NICU journey can be unexpected and challenging, it's also a place of hope, advanced medical care, and dedicated professionals working tirelessly to give each baby their best possible start in life.

CHAPTER TWENTY

PREPARING FOR THE NICU

NICU Checklist

As a NICU parent, being prepared can make a significant difference in your comfort and ability to focus on your baby. This comprehensive checklist covers everything you might need during your NICU visits, from personal-comfort items to essentials for bonding with your baby.

For Your Personal Comfort

- **Comfortable clothing:** Pack layers, as NICU temperatures can vary. Consider soft, quiet fabrics that won't disrupt the peaceful environment.

- **Footwear:** Bring slip-on shoes for easy removal when entering sterile areas.

- **Personal-care items:** Include hand sanitizer, lotion for frequent hand-washing, lip balm, and any personal medications.

- **Stress-relief items:** Pack stress balls, fidget toys, or aromatherapy rollers (if allowed).

For Extended Stays

- **Sleeping essentials:** A small travel pillow and a light blanket can make overnight stays more comfortable.

- **Entertainment:** Bring a tablet loaded with e-books, podcasts, or meditation apps. Don't forget chargers and earphones.

- **Snacks and hydration:** Pack nonperishable snacks and a reusable water bottle.

For Organization and Communication

- **NICU journal:** A dedicated notebook for tracking your baby's progress, writing questions for doctors, and recording your thoughts can be invaluable.

- **File folder:** This will help you organize important documents, care instructions, and medical information.

- **Contact list:** Keep a list of important phone numbers (e.g., NICU desk, lactation consultant, social worker) handy.

For Bonding with Your Baby

- **Soft blanket or lovey:** Check with staff about what items are allowed in the isolette.

- **Books:** Bring a selection of children's books to read aloud to your baby.

- **Family photos:** Laminate some family pictures to place near your baby's bed.

- **Breast milk–scented pad:** Some NICUs encourage leaving a pad with your scent for comfort.

For Breastfeeding/Pumping Mothers

- **Nursing bras and pads:** Comfortable, easy-access bras, and absorbent pads can make all the difference.

- **Pumping supplies:** Bring your pump, extra collection bottles, and storage bags if supplying milk.

- **Nipple cream and comfort items:** You'll be glad to have soothing gel pads or nipple shields (if needed).

- **Pumping log:** Keep a log to track milk production and feeding schedules.

For Documenting Your Journey

- **Camera or smartphone:** You'll be amazed by how many precious moments and milestones you'll want to capture.

- **Milestone cards:** Special NICU milestone cards are available for unique preemie achievements.

For Later Stages and Discharge Preparation

- **Preemie or newborn clothes:** Bring a few options for various sizes and weather conditions.

- **Going-home outfit:** Choose something special but practical for your baby's big day.

- **Car seat:** Have it properly installed and ready for the car seat test.

- **Diaper bag:** Pack one with essentials for your baby's first trip home.

Additional Considerations

- **Breast milk cooler:** This will help you transport pumped milk safely.

- **Thank you notes:** These are handy for expressing gratitude to the NICU staff.

- **Self-care items:** Face masks, hand cream, or other small luxuries can help you feel human during long NICU days.

Remember, every NICU has different policies, so always check with your hospital about what items are allowed. This checklist aims to cover all bases, ensuring you're well-prepared. Being organized can help reduce stress and allow you to focus on what's most important—bonding with your baby and participating in their care.

CHAPTER TWENTY-ONE

NAVIGATING THE NICU WITH CONFIDENCE

Here is an overview for parents on how to navigate the complex world of the NICU with confidence. It covers five essential areas:

1. **Getting to Know Your Baby's Care Team**

   - Emphasizes the importance of building relationships with the medical staff

   - Provides strategies for effective communication with doctors and nurses

   - Offers tips on how to keep track of the various healthcare professionals involved in your baby's care

   - Encourages parents to ask for clarification on medical terms and procedures

2. **Advocating for Your Baby**

- Stresses the crucial role parents play as their baby's primary advocate

- Provides guidance on how to effectively voice concerns and ask questions

- Offers advice on participating in your baby's care, including hands-on activities such as diaper changes and feeding

- Explains how to engage with doctors during rounds and request regular updates

3. **Self-Care for NICU Parents**

- Highlights the importance of parental well-being during this difficult experience

- Offers practical tips for maintaining physical health, including nutrition and rest

- Provides strategies for managing stress and emotional well-being

- Discusses the benefits of joining NICU support groups and seeking professional help if needed

4. **Bonding with Your Baby**

- Explores various ways to connect with your baby in the NICU environment

- Discusses the importance of touch, voice, and presence in your baby's development

- Provides information on kangaroo care and its benefits

- Offers creative ideas for personalizing your baby's NICU space

- Emphasizes the value of keeping a NICU journal for tracking progress and processing emotions

5. **Preparing for the Emotional Aspects**

- Discusses the nonlinear nature of NICU progress and how to cope with setbacks

- Offers strategies for celebrating small victories and milestones

- Provides guidance on building a support network of family, friends, and other NICU parents

- Discusses common emotional challenges faced by NICU parents and how to address them

The NICU Team: Who's Taking Care of Your Baby?

Your baby is being cared for by a diverse team of highly specialized medical professionals. Understanding the roles and responsibilities of each team member can help you actively and confidently participate in your baby's care.

1. **Neonatologist**

- Specializes in the care of newborns, particularly those who are premature or critically ill

- Leads the NICU team and oversees your baby's overall care plan

- Diagnoses and treats complex conditions specific to newborns

- Performs specialized procedures such as inserting central lines or intubation

- Communicates with parents about the baby's condition, treatment plans, and prognosis

2. Neonatal Nurse Practitioner (NNP)

- Advanced practice nurse with specialized training in neonatal care

- Works closely with neonatologists to manage patient care

- Can perform many procedures and sometimes leads daily rounds

- Often serves as a liaison between the medical team and parents

3. NICU Nurses

- Provide round-the-clock, hands-on care for your baby

- Monitor vital signs, administer medications, and manage feeding

- Assist with procedures and alert doctors to any changes

in the baby's condition

- Educate parents on baby-care techniques and support family involvement

- Often serve as primary nurses, providing continuity of care

4. Respiratory Therapists

- Specialize in managing breathing support for NICU babies

- Set up and monitor ventilators, CPAP machines, and other respiratory equipment

- Perform assessments of lung function and adjust oxygen levels as needed

- Educate parents on respiratory care and equipment use

5. Lactation Consultants

- Provide expert support for breastfeeding and milk expression

- Help mothers establish and maintain milk supply

- Assist with positioning and latching techniques for breastfeeding premature babies

- Offer guidance on milk storage and fortification for optimal nutrition

6. Occupational Therapists

- Focus on developing fine motor skills and sensory processing

- Work on feeding skills, including bottle- and breastfeeding

- Help babies develop appropriate responses to touch and movement

- Guide parents in appropriate developmental play and positioning

7. **Physical Therapists**

- Concentrate on gross motor development and muscle tone

- Perform exercises to prevent muscle contractures in babies with limited movement

- Teach parents techniques to support their baby's physical development

- Assist in preparing babies for developmental milestones

8. **Speech and Language Therapists**

- Specialize in feeding and swallowing issues

- Work on oral motor skills necessary for feeding

- Assist in transitioning from tube feeding to oral feeding

- Provide strategies to stimulate early communication skills

9. **Social Workers**

- Offer emotional support and counseling to families

- Help navigate hospital systems and access community resources

- Assist with financial concerns and insurance issues

- Facilitate communication between families and the medical team

10. **Case Managers**

- Coordinate care between different departments and specialists

- Plan for your baby's discharge and transition to home care

- Help arrange follow-up appointments and home health services

- Assist with insurance authorizations for specialized equipment or services

11. **Nutritionists**

- Develop specialized feeding plans to ensure optimal growth and development

- Monitor your baby's nutritional intake and adjust as needed

- Provide guidance on breast milk fortification or formula

selection

○ Educate parents on their baby's unique nutritional needs

12. **Pharmacists**

○ Prepare and manage medications specific to neonatal care

○ Monitor drug interactions and dosages

○ Provide information on medication effects and potential side effects

○ Work with the medical team to develop appropriate medication plans

13. **Developmental Specialists**

○ Assess your baby's neurological and behavioral development

○ Provide interventions to support optimal development

○ Guide parents in understanding their baby's cues and behaviors

○ Assist in creating an environment that supports developmental progress

As a parent, you are an integral part of this multidisciplinary team. Your role includes:

• Providing comfort and support to your baby through touch, voice, and presence

- Participating in your baby's care as much as possible (e.g., diaper changes, feeding, and bathing)

- Asking questions and seeking clarification on your baby's condition and care plan

- Advocating for your baby's needs and sharing your observations with the care team

- Taking care of your own physical and emotional health to be strong for your baby

Remember, each member of the NICU team brings specialized expertise to your baby's care. Don't hesitate to engage with them, ask questions, and participate actively in your baby's care. Your involvement is crucial for your baby's well-being and your own peace of mind.

What to Expect in the First Few Days

The first few days in the NICU can be overwhelming and emotionally challenging. This section provides a list of what parents can expect during this critical time:

1. Immediate Medical Interventions

- Your baby could be taken to the NICU quickly for assessment and stabilization.

- Various medical equipment will be attached to monitor vital signs and provide necessary support.

- Doctors will perform initial examinations and might order tests to determine your baby's condition.

2. Regular Medical Updates

- Expect frequent updates from doctors and nurses about your baby's condition.

- Progress may be measured in small increments, and some days might feel like setbacks.

- Learn to celebrate small victories, such as stable vital signs or small weight gains.

3. Limited Physical Contact

- Depending on your baby's condition, you might not be able to hold them immediately.

- Skin-to-skin contact (kangaroo care) might be delayed until your baby is stable.

- In the meantime, focus on gentle touch, talking, and singing to bond with your baby.

4. NICU Environment

- Familiarize yourself with the NICU layout, equipment, and protocols.

- Learn about visiting hours, hand-washing procedures, and any restrictions.

- Get to know your baby's care team and their roles.

5. Feeding Concerns

- Your baby could require tube feeding or IV nutrition

initially.

- If you plan to breastfeed, start pumping as soon as possible to establish milk supply.

- Work with lactation consultants to learn about milk storage and eventual breastfeeding techniques.

6. Emotional Rollercoaster

- Expect a wide range of emotions, from hope and joy to fear and sadness.

- It's normal to feel overwhelmed, anxious, or even detached at times.

- Don't hesitate to seek emotional support from hospital staff, family, or support groups.

7. Self-Care and Rest

- Try to establish a routine that includes rest and self-care.

- Consider staying at a nearby Ronald McDonald House if available.

- Take breaks when needed, and don't feel guilty about it.

8. Learning Medical Terminology

- You'll be introduced to many new medical terms and procedures.

- Don't be afraid to ask for explanations or clarifications from the medical team.

- Consider keeping a notebook to jot down information and questions.

9. Bonding Challenges

- Bonding might feel different than you expected due to the NICU environment.

- Focus on ways you can participate in your baby's care, such as changing diapers or taking temperatures.

- Bring personal items such family photos or soft toys (if allowed) to personalize your baby's space.

10. Preparing for the Long Haul

- Understand that the NICU stay could be longer than initially anticipated.

- Start thinking about practical matters such as parking, meals, and balancing NICU time with other responsibilities.

- Connect with other NICU parents for support and shared experiences.

Remember, every parent's experience is unique. While these first few days can be challenging, they also mark the beginning of your baby's journey toward health and strength. Don't hesitate to lean on your support system and the NICU staff during this time.

Common Equipment in the NICU

This section looks at the various equipment used in the NICU, helping parents understand the purpose and function of each device caring for their baby:

1. **Incubator/Isolette**

   ◦ **Description:** A clear plastic-enclosed bed that provides a controlled environment

   ◦ **Function:** Maintains optimal temperature, humidity, and oxygen levels

   ◦ *Example:* For a 28-week preemie, the incubator might be set at 98.6°F with 80% humidity.

2. **Ventilator**

   ◦ **Description:** A breathing machine connected to the baby through an endotracheal tube

   ◦ **Function:** Provides oxygen and helps inflate the lungs for babies unable to breathe independently

   ◦ *Example:* A baby with Respiratory Distress Syndrome might require a ventilator set to deliver 40 breaths per minute.

3. **CPAP (Continuous Positive Airway Pressure)**

   ◦ **Description:** A noninvasive breathing support system using nasal prongs or a small mask

   ◦ **Function:** Delivers a constant flow of air to keep air sacs in the lungs open

- ○ *Example:* A 34-week preemie might use CPAP set at 5 cm H2O pressure to assist with breathing.

4. Feeding Tubes (NG/OG Tubes)

- ○ **Description:** Thin, flexible tubes inserted through the nose (NG) or mouth (OG) into the stomach

- ○ **Function:** Allows direct feeding for babies unable to suck or swallow effectively

- ○ *Example:* A 2-pound preemie might receive 20 ml of breast milk every 3 hours through an NG tube.

5. IV Lines

- ○ **Description:** Tiny tubes inserted into veins, often in the hand, foot, or scalp

- ○ **Function:** Delivers fluids, medications, and nutrients directly into the bloodstream

- ○ *Example:* A preemie might receive antibiotics and TPN (Total Parenteral Nutrition) through a PICC line.

6. Pulse Oximeter

- ○ **Description:** A small sensor usually wrapped around the hand or foot

- ○ **Function:** Measures oxygen saturation in the blood and heart rate

- *Example:* Alarms might sound if a baby's oxygen levels drop below 88% or if heart rate exceeds 180 bpm.

7. **Heart Monitor**

- **Description:** Small adhesive patches on the chest connected to a monitor

- **Function:** Continuously tracks heart rate and breathing patterns

- *Example:* For a term baby, normal heart rate might range from 120 to 160 bpm.

8. **Phototherapy Lights**

- **Description:** Bright blue lights positioned over the baby or incorporated into a blanket

- **Function:** Treats jaundice by breaking down bilirubin in the skin

- *Example:* A baby with a bilirubin level of 12 mg/dL might receive phototherapy for 24–48 hours.

9. **Infusion Pumps**

- **Description:** Machines that control the delivery of fluids and medications

- **Function:** Ensures precise dosing and rate of administration for various treatments

- *Example:* A pump might be set to deliver 0.5 ml of a

medication over 30 minutes.

Celebrating NICU Milestones

As a NICU parent, your journey is unique, but that doesn't mean you can't celebrate your baby's special moments. In fact, every milestone in the NICU is a cause for celebration, no matter how small it may seem. This section explores various NICU milestones and offers creative ideas to commemorate these precious moments.

1. **First Outfit:** The day your baby wears their first outfit is a significant milestone. It often signifies that they're stable enough to be dressed, which is a big step in the NICU. To celebrate:

Remember, every NICU experience is unique, and milestones occur at different times for different babies. The key is to celebrate progress, no matter how small. These celebrations not only create lasting memories but also provide hope and motivation during challenging times.

Lastly, don't forget to celebrate yourself as a NICU parent. Your strength, resilience, and dedication are worthy of recognition. Consider treating yourself to something special after particularly challenging days or when you reach your own milestones, like your 100th day in the NICU.

By acknowledging and celebrating these moments, you're creating a positive narrative around your NICU experience, one that focuses on progress and hope. These celebrations will become cherished memories and powerful reminders of how far your little fighter has come.

Navigating NICU Rounds

One of the most intimidating aspects of the NICU experience is participating in morning rounds. As a new parent, you will find yourself surrounded by medical professionals with vast knowledge, while you stand there feeling vulnerable and trying to understand the complex medical terms, courses of action, and daily plans—all within a few brief minutes.

I vividly remember Bailey's first few rounds. I sat in the room while the medical team discussed her next steps outside, unaware that I could listen in or advocate for my baby's care. It wasn't until a compassionate nurse informed me that rounds weren't just for doctors and the medical team to discuss care, but also a time for parents to ask questions and receive updated information on next steps, that I started to join in and learn.

This section aims to demystify the rounds process and empower parents to actively participate in their baby's care:

Preparing for Rounds

1. Keep a dedicated notebook for questions and observations.

2. Review your baby's monitors and note any changes or concerns.

3. Arrive at the NICU early to get updates from the night nurse.

4. Familiarize yourself with your baby's current treatment plan

5. Prepare a list of questions or concerns to address during rounds.

What to Expect During Rounds

1. A large team of medical professionals will gather near your baby's space.

2. The discussion will typically follow a structured format, covering:

   ◦ Overnight events and current status

   ◦ Vital signs and lab results

   ◦ Nutrition and feeding plans

   ◦ Respiratory support

   ◦ Medications

   ◦ Short-term and long-term care plans

3. Medical terminology will be used frequently.

4. The team may make decisions about adjusting your baby's care plan.

Types of Questions to Ask

1. Can you explain [medical term] in simpler language?

2. What is the goal for my baby today/this week?

3. Have there been any changes to my baby's condition since yesterday?

4. What are the next milestones we're working toward?

5. Are there any new test results, and what do they mean?

6. Can you explain the risks and benefits of this treatment plan?

7. How can I be more involved in my baby's care today?

8. When might we expect to see improvements in [specific area of concern]?

9. Are there any changes to the feeding or medication plan?

10. What signs of progress or concern should I be watching for?

Tips for Effective Participation

1. Don't be afraid to speak up—your observations are valuable.

2. Ask for clarification if you don't understand something.

3. Take notes during the discussion.

4. Request a recap of the main points and action items at the end.

5. If you think of questions later, write them down for the next day's rounds.

Remember, as a parent, you are the most constant presence in your baby's life. Your involvement in rounds is crucial for understanding your baby's progress, participating in decision-making, and ensuring the best possible care for your little one.

By actively engaging in rounds, you'll not only stay informed about your baby's condition but also develop a stronger partnership with the medical team. This collaboration is vital for your baby's care and your own peace of mind throughout the NICU journey.

Don't be discouraged if it takes time to feel comfortable during rounds. With each passing day, you'll gain confidence, expand your knowledge, and become an even stronger advocate for your baby. Your dedication and involvement make a significant difference in your child's care and development in the NICU.

Partner, Family, and Sibling Support in the NICU

This section looks at the crucial aspects of supporting not just the NICU baby, but the entire family unit during this challenging time. It covers three main areas: supporting your partner, involving siblings, and setting boundaries with extended family.

1. **Supporting Your Partner:** The NICU experience can strain even the strongest relationships. This list provides practical strategies for couples to support each other:

   - **Dividing NICU visits:** Create a schedule that allows both partners time with the baby while ensuring self-care. For example, one partner might take morning shifts while the other handles evenings, or they might alternate full days.

   - **Emotional check-ins:** Set aside time each day to discuss feelings and concerns. This could be over a shared meal or during a quiet moment at home.

○ **Sharing responsibilities:** Divide tasks like pumping, sterilizing equipment, or liaising with medical staff to prevent burnout.

○ **Celebrating small victories together:** Whether it's a gram gained or a successful feed, acknowledge these moments as a team.

○ *Example:* Sarah and Tom created a shared digital calendar to coordinate NICU visits, pump schedules, and home responsibilities. They also instituted a nightly "debrief" session during which they could openly share their fears and hopes.

2. **Involving Siblings:** Helping other children understand and cope with their sibling's NICU stay is crucial. This list offers age-appropriate strategies:

○ **For young children (2–5):** Use simple explanations and play therapy. For instance, setting up a "pretend NICU" with dolls can help them better understand what's occurring in the real NICU.

○ **For school-age children (6–12):** Provide more detailed explanations and involve them in age-appropriate ways, such as drawing pictures for the baby's room.

○ **For teenagers:** Be open about the situation and allow them to visit the NICU, if possible. Encourage them to express their feelings through journaling or art.

○ *Example:* Eight-year-old Emma was feeling left out during her brother's NICU stay. Her parents involved her by asking her to create a "welcome home" banner and choose a special toy for his crib, helping her feel connected to her new sibling.

3. **Setting Boundaries with Extended Family:** While family support can be invaluable, it can also become overwhelming. This list provides guidance on managing family involvement:

○ Designating a family spokesperson to share updates, reducing the burden of constant communication

○ Setting clear visiting policies aligned with NICU rules and your comfort level

○ Tactfully addressing unhelpful advice or comments—for example, "We appreciate your concern, but we're following our doctor's recommendations"

○ Suggesting specific ways family members can help, such as preparing meals or helping with household chores

○ *Example:* When well-meaning relatives kept offering outdated childcare advice, Maria and Carlos created a weekly email update that included current best practices for preemie care, gently educating their family while keeping them informed.

Checklist: How Loved Ones Can Help a NICU Parent

This practical list offers concrete ways for family and friends to support NICU parents:

- Provide meals or grocery shopping services

- Offer to do household chores or run errands

- Listen without judgment and offer emotional support

- Help with childcare for siblings

- Organize a support network for long-term assistance

- Respect the parents' need for privacy and their visiting wishes

- Learn about NICU policies to be a more informed supporter

- Offer to be a point of contact for updating other friends and family

Preparing for Discharge

As your NICU journey nears its end, preparing for discharge becomes a crucial step in transitioning your baby from hospital to home care. This list is here to help you through this exciting yet potentially overwhelming phase.

1. **Signs Your Baby Is Ready for Discharge**

   ○ **Consistent weight gain:** Your baby should be steadily gaining weight, typically 20–30 grams per day.

- **Feeding milestones:** Successful oral feeding (breast or bottle) for most or all feeds

- **Temperature regulation:** Maintaining body temperature in an open crib

- **Breathing stability:** No apnea or bradycardia episodes for a specified period (usually 5-7 days)

2. The Car Seat Test

- **Purpose:** To ensure your baby can safely maintain their oxygen levels and heart rate while in a car seat

- **Process:** Your baby will be placed in their car seat for 90–120 minutes while connected to monitors.

- **Preparation:** Bring your car seat to the NICU a few days before the test. Ensure it's appropriate for your baby's size and weight.

- *Example:* Amanda's son failed his first car seat test due to slight oxygen desaturation. The NICU team adjusted his position with rolled towels, and he passed on the second attempt.

3. Learning Home Care Before Discharge

- **CPR training:** Both parents should complete an infant CPR course.

- **Medication management:** Practice preparing and administering any required medications.

- **Feeding techniques:** Master feeding methods, whether breastfeeding, bottle-feeding, or using feeding tubes.

- **Equipment use:** Learn how to operate and troubleshoot any necessary medical equipment.

- *Example:* Maria and Carlos spent a week rooming-in at the NICU, learning to manage their daughter's feeding tube and oxygen support under nurse supervision before discharge.

4. Preparing Your Home

- Deep-clean your house, focusing on areas where the baby will spend time.

- Set up a nursery with all necessary items within easy reach.

- Ensure proper air quality; consider air purifiers if recommended by your doctor.

- Prepare a changing station and feeding area on each floor of your home if applicable.

- *Example:* We created a "baby zone" in their living room with a portable crib, changing supplies, and feeding equipment to minimize trips up and down stairs.

5. Coordinating Follow-up Care

- Schedule appointments with your pediatrician and any specialists before discharge.

○ Arrange for home health visits if needed.

○ Understand your baby's medication schedule and refill process.

○ *Example:* Before leaving the NICU, Bobby and I had appointments set with a pediatrician, pulmonologist, and occupational therapist for the following week.

6. Emotional Preparation

○ Discuss any anxieties or concerns with the NICU staff.

○ Consider joining a support group for NICU graduates.

○ Plan for postpartum support, including mental health resources if needed.

○ *Example:* Sarah attended a "Life After NICU" workshop organized by the hospital, which helped her prepare mentally for the transition home.

7. Day of Discharge Checklist

• Collect all discharge paperwork and instructions.

• Ensure you have prescriptions for all medications.

• Pack personal items and any mementos from the NICU stay.

• Double-check you have all necessary medical equipment.

• Take final photos with NICU staff.

• Install car seat and have it checked by a certified technician.

- Pack a "go bag" with essentials for the first 24 hours at home.

- Confirm your home is prepared and stocked with supplies.

- Review emergency contact numbers and when to call the doctor.

- Take a deep breath and celebrate this milestone!

Remember, discharge day is a significant milestone, but it's normal to feel a mix of excitement and anxiety. Trust in the skills you've learned during your NICU stay, and don't hesitate to reach out to your medical team with any questions or concerns as you transition to home care. Your NICU journey has prepared you well for this next chapter in your baby's life.

Life After the NICU

The transition from the NICU to home is a significant milestone, but it comes with its own set of challenges and adjustments. This section offers tips and reminders for families ready to go home:

1. **Transitioning Home**

   ○ Emotional preparation for leaving the structured NICU environment

   ○ Setting up a home-care routine that mimics NICU schedules

   ○ Adjusting to life without constant medical monitoring

   ○ Strategies for managing anxiety about your baby's health

○ Creating a supportive home environment for your preemie

2. Managing Appointments and Follow-ups

○ Organizing a system for tracking multiple specialist appointments

○ Understanding the roles of different post-NICU specialists

○ Tips for effective communication with healthcare providers

○ Maintaining detailed records of your baby's progress

○ Balancing medical care with family life and work commitments

3. Germ Precautions and Health Management

○ Implementing strict hygiene practices at home

○ Establishing visitor rules to protect your preemie's health

○ Navigating RSV season and other seasonal health concerns

○ Recognizing signs that require immediate medical attention

○ Strategies for safely introducing your baby to the outside world

4. Feeding Challenges and Nutrition

- Transitioning from NICU feeding schedules to home routines

- Managing specialized feeding needs (e.g., fortified breast milk, special formulas)

- Addressing common feeding issues in preemies

- Working with lactation consultants and nutritionists post-discharge

- Monitoring growth and adjusting nutrition plans

5. Developmental Care and Early Intervention

- Understanding adjusted age and developmental milestones

- Implementing developmentally supportive care at home

- Recognizing signs that might require early intervention

- Learning the early intervention system and services

- Balancing therapy appointments with family life

6. Post-NICU Parent Emotions and Mental Health

- Coping with the emotional aftermath of the NICU experience

- Recognizing signs of postpartum depression and PTSD in NICU parents

- Finding support through therapy, support groups, and peer connections

- Strategies for self-care and stress management

- Nurturing your relationship with your partner post-NICU

7. Financial Management and Insurance Navigation

- Understanding insurance coverage for post-NICU care

- Managing medical bills and negotiating with providers

- Exploring financial assistance programs for NICU families

- Planning for long-term financial implications of preemie care

- Balancing work and caregiving responsibilities

8. Building Your Support Network

- Connecting with other post-NICU families

- Utilizing online resources and support groups

- Educating friends and family about your preemie's unique needs

- Finding respite care and trustworthy childcare options

- Celebrating milestones and creating new family traditions

A Final Note

If you've made it this far, thank you. I hope my story made you feel seen and gave you hope, and I hope this guide gives you the support and confidence you need to get through your own NICU journey.

The NICU is a world of its own, filled with anxiety and worry. Something I didn't even know about until after giving birth to Bailey. But it is also a magical place, and it is your baby's first home.

This season will always be part of your story, but it won't always feel as heavy as it does right now. One day, you'll look back and see just how strong you and your baby truly were.

Until then, keep holding on to the little victories, keep giving yourself grace, and know that you are not walking this road alone.

With love and understanding,

Another NICU Mom

Chapter Twenty-Two

NICU Glossary: Common Medical Terms for Parents

T he NICU can feel like an entirely different world, filled with unfamiliar machines, abbreviations, and medical terms. Understanding these terms can help you feel more informed and confident in your baby's care.

How to Use This Glossary

- Keep this glossary handy during NICU visits.

- If you hear a term you don't understand, ask your baby's care team to explain it.

- Understanding these terms will help you feel more confident in conversations with doctors and nurses.

A–C

- **Apgar score:** A quick assessment of a newborn's health immediately after birth, scoring on heart rate, breathing, muscle tone, reflexes, and color.

- **Apnea:** When a baby temporarily stops breathing for more than 20 seconds. Common in preemies.

- **Bilirubin:** A substance in the blood that can cause jaundice (yellowing of the skin). High levels can require phototherapy.

- **Bradycardia ("brady"):** A drop in heart rate, common in preemies. Often seen with apnea episodes.

- **CPAP (Continuous Positive Airway Pressure):** A machine that helps keep a baby's airways open with gentle air pressure. Air is pushed through a mask on the baby's face.

D–F

- **Desaturation ("desat"/"desatting"):** A drop in oxygen levels in the blood, often triggering an alarm.

- **Endotracheal tube (ET tube):** A tube placed in the baby's airway to assist with breathing via a ventilator.

- **Extubation:** The process of removing a baby from a ventilator when they can breathe on their own.

- **Fortifier:** Extra nutrients (including protein and calories)

added to breast milk or formula to help a preemie gain
weight.

G–I

- **Gavage feeding:** Feeding a baby through a tube in the nose
  or mouth when they are not ready for bottle or breastfeeding.

- **Gestational age:** The number of weeks a baby has been in
  the womb before birth. A full-term baby is born at 37–40
  weeks.

- **Hematocrit (HCT):** A measure of red blood cells in the
  blood, which is important for carrying oxygen.

- **High-flow nasal cannula (HFNC):** A type of oxygen therapy that delivers slightly pressurized air through small tubes
  in the nose.

- **Incubator/isolette:** A temperature-controlled bed that
  helps regulate a preemie's body temperature.

J–P

- **Jaundice:** A common condition in newborns in which the
  skin and eyes appear yellow due to high bilirubin levels. Often treated with phototherapy.

- **Kangaroo care:** Skin-to-skin contact between a parent
  and baby, which helps regulate temperature, breathing, and

bonding.

- **Meconium:** A baby's first stool, which is thick and dark green.

- **Nasogastric (NG) tube:** A feeding tube that passes through the nose into the stomach to provide direct nutrition.

- **Oxygen hood:** A small plastic hood placed over a baby's head to provide extra oxygen.

- **Patent Ductus Arteriosus (PDA):** A condition where a small vessel in the heart doesn't close after birth, which often requires monitoring or treatment.

- **Phototherapy:** Light therapy used to treat jaundice in newborns.

R–Z

- **Respiratory Distress Syndrome (RDS):** A common breathing condition in preemies due to underdeveloped lungs.

- **Retinopathy of prematurity (ROP):** An eye condition (also common) affecting preemies due to abnormal blood vessel growth in the eyes.

- **Sepsis:** A serious infection in the bloodstream that can be dangerous for newborns.

- **Surfactant:** A substance that helps keep a baby's lungs open and makes breathing easier. Often given to preemies with RDS.

- **Tachycardia:** A fast heart rate.

- **Tachypnea:** Rapid breathing, often a sign of lung immaturity.

- **Ventilator:** A machine that helps babies breathe when they cannot do so on their own.